Baseball's 6th Tool

The Inner Game

John D. Curtis, Ph.D.

Foreword by Jamie Moyer

By the time I'm 60 I want to:
1. Never have missed anything with my family
2. Financially secure so that if I pass away my family will not have financial concern
3. Deepen my relationship with Christ

3/1/13

baseballs6thtool.com
La Crosse, Wisconsin

ISBN 978-0-9822760-2-0

Printed in the United States of America

*Dedicated to
Frank Bartenetti and
the late Harvey Dorfman,
friends, mentors and
pioneers in the field of
personal coaching.*

Acclaim for Baseball's 6th Tool

"Jack Curtis has taken his work and vision and put it into a wonderfully written book every athlete should read, then take the principles and work them. The mental part of the game is what separates the great ones. I know personally the mental part was missing from my career . . . as well as my life. *Baseball's 6th Tool* is a difference-maker."

—Dickie Noles, *Employee Assistance Professional, Philadelphia Phillies; 11-year MLB career*

"Jack is an expert on the 'mental game' and has been a big influence in my career. He has the unique ability to help people identify what's holding them back and then assist them in developing a plan to overcome these blocks. The skills presented in this book would benefit everyone."

—Jim Murphy, *Author of Inner Excellence, Performance Coach*

"In *Baseball's 6th Tool: The Inner Game,* Dr. Curtis provides a common-sense approach to prepare players for the rigors of competition. Both players and coaches will benefit from the annotated exercises to help affirm and visualize performance and reinforce a positive mindset. Having used the skills from Jack's first book, *The Mindset for Winning,* I can testify to their value. I'm a believer!"

—Tom O'Connell, *National High School Coaches Association Coach of the Year, 2011: American Baseball Coaches Association (ABCA) National Coach of the Year, 2004, 2005; MLB Lead Envoy Coach to Germany since 1993*

"Jack's earlier book, The Mindset for Winning, became the foundation for the mental and emotional skills training we do with our players. His latest book, *Baseball's 6th Tool: The Inner Game,* is a valuable resource. I believe the strength of an athlete's inner game ultimately determines his career success."

—Todd Oakes, *Pitching Coach, University of Minnesota, 12 years in the San Francisco Giants organization*

"*Baseballs 6th Tool* is the best, most realistic, and practical baseball book to reach coaches I've seen. It doesn't get any better than this."

—Joseph R. Caligure, *Former Head Coach, Western Oregon University*

Table of Contents

PART 1: The Way to Proceed................................. 5

Chapter 1   A Little Difference Makes a Major Difference 7

Chapter 2   The Winning Mindset................................ 17

Chapter 3   Limiting Performance 33

Chapter 4   Your Powerful Mind 41

PART 2: Laying the Foundation for Change 51

Chapter 5   The Evaluation Process 53

Chapter 6   Goals: Your Blueprint for Success................. 67

PART 3: The Four Basic Mental Skills 81

Chapter 7   Relaxation: The Power of Letting Go 85

Chapter 8   Activating Your Left Brain:
            The Affirmation Process........................... 101

Chapter 9   Mental Recall: Activating Your Right Brain 115

Chapter 10 Mental Rehearsal 127

PART 4: Applying the Mental Game 137

Chapter 11 Making It Yours 139

Chapter 12 Confidence....................................... 151

Chapter 13 Improving Concentration:
            You Must Be Present to Win........................ 161

Chapter 14 The Mental Game for Injured Players 169

EPILOGUE 178

APPENDICES 179

Appendix A: Psychological Development Form (PDF)......... 179

Appendix B: Standard Autogenic Training 187

Appendix C: Mental Recall Worksheet 189

Foreword

*B*aseball's *6th Tool* is a fantastic read for those who want to better themselves as athletes and as people. As you read this book, you'll learn that being able to change a behavior (your behavior) will allow you to achieve more consistent performance. Your challenge is to learn the mental skills and apply them.

Creating a mental game plan is so very important to an athlete's success. Over many years of mental preparation, physical preparation, experience, success, and failure, I have come to the conclusion that without the right tools and the skills to apply them, you may never reach your full potential as an athlete or a person.

The types of skills presented in this book are what I have used over my long career. I'm familiar with many of the concepts because of my relationship with Harvey Dorfman. I miss him dearly. Jack also knew Harvey well, as a friend and mentor, and while his ideas are similar and build on what I learned from Harvey, they also energized me even more as I approach the upcoming season. I found the book both educational and refreshing to read, and I will definitely use the techniques presented in it. *Baseball's 6th Tool* is proof you can teach an old dog new tricks.

I'm giving copies of the book to both of my sons, who are eligible for the draft this year. This book will help any aspiring or current athlete to strengthen their mental game or to overcome mental hurdles.

—Jamie Moyer

Jamie Moyer's 23-year major league career spans four decades. He won the 2008 World Series Championship with the Philadelphia Phillies. A former All-Star, Jamie has won 267 major league games to date, and, at age 49, he is striving for a comeback after arm surgery in 2011.

Introduction

"There is nothing new under the sun."

King Solomon, Ecclesiastes 1:9

I've been blessed to have the opportunity to work with professional baseball players for 16 years, and I cherish and have learned much from this experience. Over the years I've met many players who have never reached their potential, and it's certainly not due to lack of effort. They have the work ethic, the desire and the will to excel, but something is missing that prevents them from consistently performing at their best. This book is about that "missing something."

As players you will be confronted with many stressors that can affect your game. Fear of failure, the pressure to win and the need to impress are just a few issues you must overcome before you can bring your best to the park each day. Too often these internal struggles take the joy out of competition. This book is also about bringing the joy back into your game, and, along the way, releasing your true inner potential.

I've learned that although players are unique, there are also many similarities between them as they travel what is often a parallel route. All professional players have the same destination in mind, but what they experience along the journey and how they respond to like situations is definitely individual.

Yet within these differences there is one constant. Players play their best when they are confident. This book will focus on what I consider to be the basics of success on the field — confidence and consistency. The two go hand in hand. Without complete inner confidence, you cannot perform consistently. Without consistency, you will never reach your true potential.

The foundation of success is confidence, and confidence comes from your inner beliefs, your self-image. Years of research have concluded that you can't outperform your self-image. Therefore, the focus of the book will be on strengthening your inner beliefs so that you enter each game confident regardless of previous outcomes. It's your inner beliefs that will carry you through both good times and bad, and trust me, there will be struggles along the way. Your challenge is to meet each one successfully.

The Intent

The challenge for me was to keep the book relevant and manageable. There is so much more that I wanted to add, but in an effort to keep it applicable, I've tried to identify the key concepts that affect performance and provide insight on how to use this information successfully without overwhelming you. I only hope the information selected paints a clear picture for you.

As you begin reading you'll probably find that the book is much like starting a giant jigsaw puzzle. You may not see how things relate at the onset, but as you move through each chapter, the picture will become clearer, and by the end you'll have a more complete picture of the mental approach to baseball. The material presented is designed to help you reframe your thinking and take your game to the next level.

My intent is threefold:

1. To emphasize the importance of applying the mental game (if you don't already recognize its significance).

2. To illustrate how simple it is to implement the mental game into your daily routine.

3. To stimulate your interest to explore the topic further and to expand your knowledge through other sources such as the many excellent books available on the topic.

I'd like to emphasize that by no means is this an exhaustive book on baseball's mental game, nor is it designed to replace other books on this topic. This book will approach the mental game from a completely different viewpoint than other books do.

King Solomon's quote opening this introduction said it best. "There is nothing new under the sun." Nothing I say in this book is new or original to me. I don't even want to insinuate that I've discovered anything new. I'm just taking the information already discovered and applying it from a different perspective. Hopefully this perspective can help simplify the topic and make it more valuable to you as a player.

The Approach

I am not a trained sports psychologist, but I have been working with Olympic, national and professional athletes on their mental game before sports psychology was recognized as a science. I guess you could say I am truly "grandfathered in."

My educational background is in the field of health science, and the foundational principles of my profession will be reflected throughout the book. The emphasis of health science as a profession is threefold. First, viewing things from the total person or "holistic" standpoint; second, taking theory and academic research, simplifying it and applying it to everyday life; and third, teaching how to change behaviors.

The first of these, viewing everything from the total-person standpoint, means we are multi-dimensional beings. We are not only physical beings, but we are also emotional, social, intellectual and spiritual beings. These five dimensions cannot be separated. What affects one dimension affects all the dimensions — the total person.

In baseball the focus often becomes very one dimensional — physically dominated — and everything evolves around the physical at the expense of the other dimensions. When players become too one dimensional, not only does performance on the field suffer, but life away from the field suffers as well. It's important to maintain balance in your life between all five dimensions.

The second focus of health science involves taking theory and academic information and simplifying it for the layperson. I'll do my best to explain things in a simple, practical and relevant way. In fact, chapters are purposely kept short and the book has been broken into four parts to make it more user friendly.

The third focus of health science is to apply relevant information to your life. This involves changing behavior. Much of my training was on teaching people to change behaviors quickly and permanently. You will see all three of these foundation principles carried throughout the book.

The mental game is not complex, and I will not try to make it so. You don't need to know the intricate details of how your mind is wired, nor do you need an advanced degree in psychology to understand and use the mental game to your benefit. Keep your mental game simple. Adapt it, add to it, and delete from it to meet your needs. There is no right way or wrong way in applying the mental game. The right way is the one that works for you.

Remember, "The road to success is always under construction." Enjoy the journey.

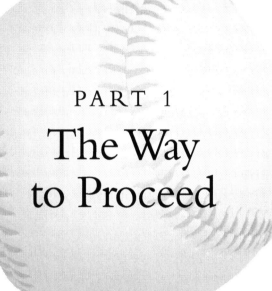

PART 1

The Way to Proceed

Have you ever been frustrated because you know you are better than you've been playing? This is a common problem faced by most players, and in Part 1 you will learn how and why this occurs. Part 1 sets the stage for those that follow.

Here I'll explain how your enormous potential has been held in check because of your previously established inner beliefs, some of which are false. Once you come to understand that foundational principle, you will learn how you can use the same principles that established these false beliefs to take your performance to a higher level on a consistent basis.

In this section of the book you will learn how your brain works and how you can use it to your advantage. Your brain is a powerful tool that can work for you or against you depending on the input you provide. If the input is poor, you create mental barriers to your success. When this occurs you establish a false ceiling that limits your success and prevents you from playing at a high level on a consistent basis.

Read Part 1 with an open mind as you are introduced to a new way of thinking and shown how this can unleash your potential. It may not be much different than your current way of thinking, but making subtle changes can make a major difference in your career path.

CHAPTER 1

A Little Difference Makes a Major Difference

"It's not what you've got, it's what you use that
makes a difference."

Zig Ziglar

Baseball is more than pitching, hitting and fielding. For all its physical effort, baseball is a mental game.

The importance of the mental game was emphasized by Hall of Famer Yogi Berra, who said, "Baseball is 90 percent mental. The other 50 percent is physical." Maybe Yogi's math was lacking, but he certainly knew the significance of the mental game. So does Charlie Manuel, manager of the Philadelphia Phillies. In a recent interview, Manuel emphasized the magnitude of the mental game and simply stated, "Baseball is 90 percent mental."

Baseball is a mental game. Why should you care? Because it affects your career, that's why!

As you read this book, you'll learn more about the mental game of baseball. In addition, I will introduce you to some simple yet powerful techniques you can add to your daily routine to help you perform not only at a higher level but also at a more consistent level.

Performance and consistency: That's what the mental game can do for you. It complements your physical skills and turns your potential into performance on the diamond.

What Makes a Great Baseball Player?

In 1987, Tom Trebelhorn, who at that time was the manager of the Milwaukee Brewers, gave me my first opportunity to work with players at the major league level. One day he described his theory on the difference between a great player and an average player: It's not that great players have so much more talent. Often average players have just as much raw talent. The difference is in consistency. Great players have learned to play consistently in the upper third of their talent level. The performance of average players fluctuates greatly. Average players tend to play great for a week or two and follow those up periods with down periods that offset these great weeks.

I've heard similar opinions expressed by others throughout my years in the sport. Many coaches have expressed their belief that the only difference between major league players and upper–minor league players (AA, AAA and those described as 4A players) is not talent, but a lack of consistency.

Figure 1-1 illustrates what Trebelhorn voiced. He could speak with authority since he witnessed greatness on a day-to-day basis. Two of his players at the time, Robin Yount and Paul Molitor, have since been inducted into baseball's Hall of Fame.

FIGURE 1-1

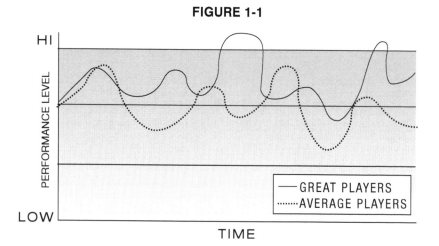

The Proper Mental State for Consistency

If your goal is to perform in the upper third of your ability level on a regular basis, your first question must be, "How can I increase my consistency?" The answer to this question requires an understanding of the two mental states that determine consistent performance. Note I said mental states: You don't get into the zone by working harder physically. If this were the case, you could work your way into that state. And as you already know, working doesn't work.

The Zone or the "Locked-In State"

You've experienced what it is to be "in the zone" or be "locked in" at various times in your career, and you would love to play in this state on a daily basis. When you've been in the zone or locked in — or

> *When I'm going good, I'm simply unconscious.*
>
> HALL OF FAMER
> GEORGE BRETT

whatever you personally call this condition — chances are you would describe it somewhat differently than others do, but you would probably use some common descriptive phrases: "I was lost in the moment," "My mind was clear and I was not thinking," "I was playing the game on automatic pilot." Hall of Famer George Brett stated, "When I'm going good, I'm simply unconscious," and Hall of Famer Ozzie Smith described this state by saying, "When I'm in my groove, there is no thinking. Everything just happens."

I wish I could tell you that the sixth tool will teach you to place yourself into this state, but I can't. The zone is one that you slip into and out of without thought. When all conditions are lined up, it just happens, as if all of the stoplights are green before you even leave home. You don't know why it happens, but you sit back and enjoy the ride — or you should. Enjoy it and ride it for as long as you can. The zone is a non-thinking state. If you try to analyze it or focus on it, you lose it immediately.

FIGURE 1-2

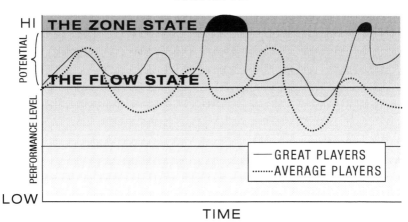

The Flow State

But there's good news. The state preceding "the zone" is under your control. The flow state is where you play in the upper third of your ability level on a consistent basis, and when you're in this state, you are close to being in the zone, where you are doing everything right from the mental standpoint.

The state of flow increases your chances of moving into the zone on a more regular basis. And when you're not quite in the zone, you still play more confidently and at a more consistently high level on a day-to-day basis. This is a state you can control and a state that will take your game to a whole new level.

A Little Difference Makes a Major Difference

Baseball, like most sports, is a game where a little difference, or a slight shift, can make a dramatic difference. Last May I was speaking with a player who had been at bat just over 100 times. He was frustrated and described himself as being "horseshit." I asked him if he would still describe himself that way if he had five more hits. His answer was yes until I mentioned that with five more hits, he would be hitting .300 — which would be above his career average.

For position players who bat 500 times a season, one hit a week or four per month throughout the season is the difference between .250 and .300. Stop and think about that. Four hits a month. It's a little difference, but it has a big impact on a career. And say you're a pitcher — it is the small difference that matters for you too. Giving up one extra run every 27 outs is the difference between a 3.0 and a 4.0 ERA. It's making that one pitch when you need it, every nine innings.

The goal of this book is to provide you with tools you need to identify the thought patterns that prevent you from being in the flow state on a regular basis. Once we identify them, we'll explore techniques and skills to help you reframe your thinking so that you can replace negative patterns with positive patterns that have the potential to make that little difference.

The Game Plan

Changing Habits Takes Time

I have found through experience that the most effective way to change habits is to take your time. I recommend that you work through this book slowly, in the sequence presented, and perform the suggested exercises in the progression presented. Permanent change takes time. If you rush the process, you may see benefits quickly, but most often the change will be short lived, and you will soon drift back to your old, limiting habits. The following is an example of such a scenerio:

Matajura wanted to become a great swordsman, but his father said he wasn't quick enough and could never learn. So Matajura went to the famous dueler, Banzo, and asked to become his pupil. "How long will it take me to become a master?" he asked. "Suppose I become your servant, was with you every minute; how long?"

"Ten years," said Banzo.

"My father is getting old. Before ten years have passed I will have to return home to take care of him. Suppose I work twice as hard; how long will it take me?"

"Thirty years," said Banzo.

"How is that?" asked Matajura. "First you say ten years. Then when I offer to work twice as hard, you say it will take three times as long. Let me make myself clear: I will work unceasingly. No hardship will be too much. How long will it take?"

"Seventy years," said Banzo. "A pupil in such a hurry learns slowly."[1]

It took time to develop your existing habits, so it will also take time to replace those old habits with new ones. Research indicates that changing any behavior takes a minimum of 14 days and as many as 40 days, assuming you are working the change every day. That being said, I have worked with athletes all my life, and I know many of you will want to get started immediately. If you truly feel the need to get started immediately, you may want to begin with Part 3, which walks you through each step of the change process. If you do choose to do so, I encourage you to read Parts 1 and 2 while you are "working the program."

Think of the mental game as a jigsaw puzzle. If you want to see the completed picture, you need to have all the pieces in place. As you assemble this puzzle, you will see how the pieces tie together, and you can better understand and identify behaviors that may be limiting your performance.

Adapt as Necessary

It's been said there are three truths in the world — your truth, my truth and the truth. We all see the world through tinted glasses. Each person has his or her own perspective, totally unique to the individual. Your experiences are as unique to you as mine are to me. Your background, education, family and cultural experiences are different. Additionally each individual interprets experiences differently.

Take what works for you and discard the rest. Pick, choose and adapt the lessons you find here so that, in the end, the plan is truly yours and works for you in your current situation. At the same time, be sure to try each technique and give it time to work. Habits, like plants, need time to germinate, and it is too easy to discard ideas because they don't agree with your current thinking. You may well need to grow into them.

The Answers Are Within

Your Task — Stop Searching and Commit

In his book *The Song of the Bird,* Anthony de Mello, S.J., tells a marvelous story called "The Little Fish."

"Excuse me," said an ocean fish. "You are older than I, so can you tell me where to find this thing they call the ocean?"

"The ocean," said the older fish, "is the thing you are in now."

"Oh, this? But this is water. What I'm seeking is the ocean," said the disappointed fish as he swam away to search elsewhere. [2]

Too often we spend time searching for something when we're still unaware just what that something is. The fact is, you already have the answers. They lie within you as you read this. I'm sure you've already suspected as much.

You've experienced periods in your game when you dominated — when the physical and mental game came together and you were in the proverbial zone. The problem is that you don't know how you got there. If you did, you'd be there all the time. It was not your physical game that put you in that state. You work the physical game every day, so if it was simply a matter of physical effort, you could place yourself into the zone state anytime you felt good and worked hard. You know that doesn't work.

I'm sure you suspect the mental game plays an important part in entering the zone state. Like most players you've probably dabbled in aspects of the mental game from time to time. Odds are you never made a decision to seriously commit to developing that part of your game. Maybe you didn't know how. Maybe you didn't think it would really work — and a half-hearted commitment never works. When the first roadblock shows up (i.e., "My family is visiting," "My agent was in town," "I was too busy," etc.) that commitment gets buried under a pile of excuses. Of course you'd never skip practice or games for these reasons. You need to make the same commitment to your mental game as you do to your physical game.

You Already Use the Mental Game

Let's get one thing straight at the onset. You already know how to use the mental game. You've done it all your life, and it has worked for you — it got you exactly where you are today. Now, if you want to take your game to a higher level, you need to stop searching and start applying what you already know — but with a revised game plan and a serious commitment to working this new plan.

That's where this book comes in. It will provide a simple plan that you can use to change your thought pattern and attitude. It will help you identify and eliminate beliefs that have limited your performance and help you develop a new attitude.

My Role

Working a plan is easier with a partner. That's why in the following pages I will:

1. Provide insights on the mental game of baseball.

2. Explain what happens in your mind, why, and how to use this information to your benefit.

3. Motivate you to make the necessary changes to elevate your performance.

Your Role

Your role will be to:

1. Make a commitment to developing your mental game (and stick with it).

2. Read with an open mind.

3. Identify past ways of thinking that have limited your performance and close the door on them, no matter how comfortable they may be.

4. Take responsibility for all of your behaviors — no excuses!

5. Apply what you learn.

As the Nike commercial says, "Just do it!"

In Sum...

- The mental game is designed to complement your physical skills.

- It's designed to place you in the "flow state," where you perform consistently in the upper 1/3 of your talent level.

- The "flow state" precedes the proverbial "zone state."

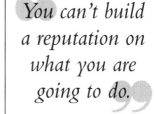

You can't build a reputation on what you are going to do.

HENRY FORD

- When performing in the "flow state," you are closer to "the zone" and will experience it more often.

- Minor shifts in your mental game can make a major impact on your performance.

- To make positive changes permanent, you need to have a solid game plan. Don't rush the process, commit to change, be open to new ideas, and work on it daily just as you do now with your physical game.

CHAPTER 2

The Winning Mindset

*"The best way to predict your future
is to create it."*

Stephen Covey

I was standing next to the batting cage at a major league park when a young player approached me. "Give me something to make me feel like I'm back in Huntsville," he said. Unfortunately, he was preparing for his major league debut later that evening, and by the look in his eyes and the desperate tone in his voice, it was obvious he wasn't prepared for that next step. He wasn't going to pitch in an AA park that night; he was in the big leagues now, and he wasn't prepared to take his game to that level.

I had never worked with that pitcher before, but I'd observed him for three years. I'd watched him dominate at all levels in his rapid ascent to the big leagues. He had tremendous talent, was rated high on baseball's five-tool system, and his talent had carried him quickly through the minor leagues. However, he had neglected to develop the most important skill he needed for long-term success in the major leagues — the foundation he needed to display his talent on baseball's biggest stage. His evening was short and, unfortunately, so was his career. He never recovered from the battering his psyche took that evening.

This is just one example, an extreme example, of a player who's not ready to play at his potential. He had all the talent, all the physical tools, but he'd never struggled in the minor leagues. Success came to him easily — maybe too easily — and he never needed to develop his mental game to complement his physical talent.

Falling Short of Your Potential

The aforementioned young pitcher is certainly not alone. We've all fallen short of fulfilling our potential. Regardless of how successful you've been, at some time during your career, you've been frustrated because you know you haven't played up to your potential. You know you have the talent to play at a higher level, and you've done everything imaginable to unleash your talent.

You have set goals and outworked your teammates. You're driven and have the passion and the desire to be great. You get "locked in" for short periods or maybe even for extended periods, but you can't sustain that momentum. You constantly tweak your game — but at the end of the day (or the year), the results are the same. You've seen other players with less talent excel. They seem to get all the breaks and all the accolades. It's as if your foot is on the gas and you're revving your engine — but it feels like the parking brake is on. How do you release it?

The process is not as daunting as you might imagine. You won't even need to make any major changes — only a slight shift in your approach.

You've been successful because 95 to 98 percent of your behavior has been correct. Those skills got you where you are today. It's the behaviors that fall into the remaining 2 to 5 percent that have placed a false ceiling on your talent, thus capping your success. It is only this small percent of your behaviors that needs to be identified and addressed.

I want to reiterate: We're not talking about making major changes. You don't need a complete makeover. What I'm suggesting is that you make minor changes mentally, much like you do when you are tweaking your delivery or your swing. It's these minor changes that can make a major difference in your results.

Potential vs. Performance

Let's consider *potential* versus *performance* to help us better understand the approach we will be taking. The whole purpose of using the information you are learning while reading this book is for you to close the gap between your current performance and your true potential.

Figure 2-1 is a simple diagram that illustrates how potential — your God-given talent — is prevented from being released. On the top, Line A represents your potential. Below that, Line B indicates the false ceiling that prevents you from reaching your potential.

This invisible ceiling is what you must break through to play up to your potential. So what is this false ceiling? What is it made of? One word: Beliefs. What's holding you back are the false beliefs you've developed over the years. These beliefs shape your current habits, attitudes, behaviors and expectations — all of which combine to make

FIGURE 2-1

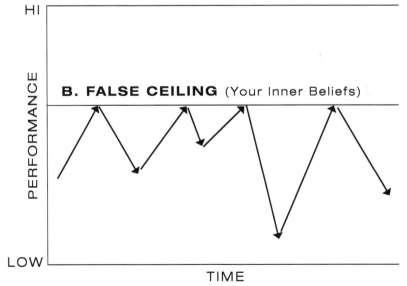

up your self-concept. It's these beliefs that cap your performance and prevent you from playing up to your potential. No matter what you do, you can't outplay these inner beliefs, your self-concept. But you can change it, and you must change it before you can permanently expand your success zone (SZ).

The goal of the mental game is to raise this invisible ceiling and close the gap between your potential and your performance.

Release the Brakes: Cover All the Bases

Abraham Lincoln once stated, "If I had eight hours to chop down a tree, I would spend the first six hours sharpening the axe." He was referring to sharpening *both* edges of the axe head, not just one. Sharpening both edges of your baseball skills is how you release the brakes.

Hold onto the mental image of this axe as you think about how you've trained and prepared for your career in baseball. The prevailing practice in the sport is to focus the majority of time and effort on physical preparation, with little or no time spent on the mental game. How many times have you told yourself "more is better" as you spent countless hours on the field or in the gym. "More is better" is one expensive attitude — one that costs you hours of time as you hone the physical side of your axe while you neglect what is possibly the most important side, the mental edge.

Sure, when you focus on sharpening the physical edge, you may still get the job done, but over the years it will take more time and a greater effort to continue to achieve than it would if you start to sharpen both edges of the blade. Total preparation — in baseball vernacular, "covering all the bases" — is the best way to get the job done quickly, effectively and with less effort.

Sharpening the mental side of your blade is how you can set yourself apart from the 90 percent of players who only focus on sharpening their physical skills. And just as you have a physical strengthening plan, you need a mental strengthening plan to excel. You must apply the correct approach and implement changes properly and consistently.

If your baseball career has followed a typical path, chances are your exposure to the mental game has been your coaches' advice to "focus better," "concentrate more," "be more relaxed," "attack the strike zone," "be more patient at the plate," "be more confident," or "get yourself ready mentally." Sound familiar? These techniques may help you regain focus, relax and such, but they are all surface skills. They don't address the root cause of your stress, lack of confidence or inability to maintain focus in the first place. Even if you perfect these techniques, they will only help you in the short term, and at the end of the year, you will find yourself with the same old results.

The skills and techniques mentioned above all play an important part in a mental game plan. I introduce them to players on a regular basis, but they fall short on their own. Techniques alone are not a mental skills program. You need to change from within by altering your inner beliefs — your self-concept — if you really want to turn your potential into performance on the field. And it all starts with your attitude.

The Power of Attitude

We've known since ancient times that the mind is a powerful force, and that your thinking is directly related to your performance. In discussing how to put one's old life behind and to take on a new nature, the Bible (Ephesians 4:23) states, "…be made new in the attitude of your minds." In other words, change your thinking to change your behavior.

In the third century A.D. Marcus Aurelius said, "Your life is what your thoughts make it." William James, considered the father of American psychology, stated, "The greatest discovery of my generation is that a human being can alter his life by altering his attitude." More recently Norman Vincent Peale stated, "Change your thoughts and you change your world."

Success is a state of mind. And when you change your pattern of thinking, your attitude changes and your performance follows.

Thoughts Dictate Actions

Prior to games, your thoughts create images in your mind. These images affect your confidence, psyching you up or psyching you out. If the images border on negative, they create anxiety, stress, lower self-confidence and lowered expectations. Conversely, when the thoughts and images are positive, they raise your confidence, enhance your self-image, make you feel successful and relaxed, and actually enhance your chances of performing better on the field. In essence, your focus determines your future. These are not my thoughts. Research documents that:

1. People perform consistently at the level of their beliefs.

2. Beliefs can be altered.

3. You alter your thoughts and beliefs by controlling what you input.

4. Taking ownership of your thoughts is how you change them.

Coaches have told you countless times you need to "control what you can control and not worry about the rest." This is exactly what the mental game provides for you — control. When you take control, you are taking ownership for the way you think, and you stop being a victim of your own mind.

Your thinking is the one thing you have 100 percent control over. Take that control; take ownership of your thoughts. You can't control the weather, what your coaches think or how teammates play, but in all these situations you can control your thoughts and thus your reaction to them — if you choose to do so.

Imagine, if you will, playing in the 9th inning of the 7th game of the World Series. The game is in the balance, and the outcome likely depends on your performance. In addition to the thousands

of screaming fans in the stands, millions are watching on ⊥ .
in reality, there is just you and your thoughts. If you have negative
thoughts and imagine failure, you'll be timid, anxious, stressed and
overwhelmed by the situation. In this instance the possibility of having
a quality performance is highly unlikely. On the other hand, if your
thoughts are positive and you imagine yourself being successful, you'll
embrace the situation with confidence and increase your chances of
success. If this is your mindset, you may not be successful every time
you face adversity, but you'll get the moniker of being a gamer and a
clutch player.

Let's examine the benefits of taking control of your thinking.

The Two Benefits of a Solid Mental Game

Your mental approach, when implemented properly, will provide you with two distinct benefits to your performance. The first
is a great improvement in your confidence level, which is a result of
strengthening your self-image. The second is creating proper muscle
memory so you can execute more consistently.

Strengthening the Self-Image Cycle

Figure 2-2 illustrates the self-image success cycle, which lays the
foundation for the confidence you have on the field. Note how this
cycle begins with your thought process, with thinking and self-talk
listed at the top. When you think positively, it influences your attitude — you expect good things to happen. You work hard because
energy follows thoughts, and that higher energy level tends to help
your practice behaviors to be more consistent. This in turn creates
improved performance, which leads to a higher level of confidence,
and this feeds the cycle with more positive thoughts and self-talk.
Once you initiate this cycle, it takes on a life of its own. It becomes
self-perpetuating.

Conversely, Figure 2-3 illustrates what happens when your
thoughts are negative. Your attitude suffers and your expectations are

FIGURE 2-2

THE SUCCESS CYCLE

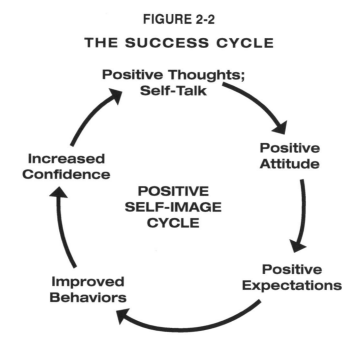

lowered and this, in turn, lowers your energy level, which causes your practice behaviors to suffer and leads to an inconsistent and lower level of performance — eroding your self-confidence even further. When this downward cycle picks up momentum, it acts like a snowball rolling downhill, getting bigger as it goes.

Thoughts have a corresponding emotion. Emotions such as fear, shame, disappointment, anger and frustration lead to lower energy levels. Thoughts that convey a positive emotion lead to increased confidence, happiness, relaxation and self-esteem. It's not the thoughts alone that determine how you react and play in specific situations; it's the emotions they generate that dictate what happens.

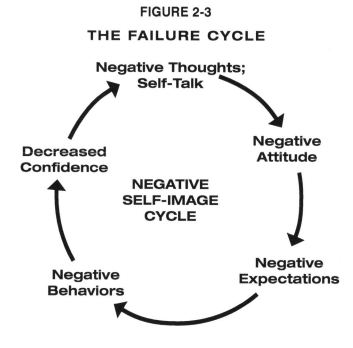

FIGURE 2-3

THE FAILURE CYCLE

Building Muscle Memory
===

The second way in which a solid mental game plan augments performance is through the influence it has on your neuromuscular system. Vivid mental images actually enhance muscle memory. Your body responds to the image in your mind, not only at the muscular level but also in the nervous system. When you visualize a movement, you map a neuromuscular pattern that will increase the chance of repeating the movement you imagined. This process is called subliminal motor movement.

This powerful concept can bring you consistent performance — or cause inconsistent performance if you don't take control of it. To demonstrate just how sensitive subliminal motor movement can be, take time now to do a Chevreul's Pendulum (instructions follow). Even if you've done it before, do it now to emphasize the mind/body connection. This fascinating and graphic illustration of the mind/ body connection illustrates how visualization, regardless of where you do it, can improve or hinder performance on the field.

Your Turn: Chevreul's Pendulum

For this technique, you'll need a pendulum, or you'll need to make one. Get a 12" to 15" piece of thin string or thread and a paper clip or a ring. Tie the object to the end of the string.

- Sit comfortably in a chair and hold one end of the string between your thumb and forefinger in your dominant hand. Lean forward, rest your elbow on your knee and relax (this is important). Place your elbow on your knee and be sure your arm is at a 45-degree angle. Keep your eyes open and look at the pendulum.

- Watch the pendulum and continue to relax by focusing your attention on the exhalation phase of your breathing. In your mind, visualize the pendulum swinging toward you and away from you (A toward you, and B away from you, Figure 2-4). Do not physically try to move it.

- After the pendulum begins to swing in the direction you imagined, change direction. Imagine it now going side to side (C-D in Figure 2-4).

- After it begins to swing freely side to side, imagine it swinging in a circle. Once you have it swinging in a circle, stop and focus on how your mind controls your most minute actions.

FIGURE 2-4

CHEVRUEL'S PENDULUM

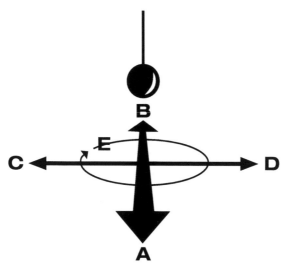

Chevreul's Pendulum illustrates how powerfully your body reacts with the subliminal motor response to the imagined movement. If you did the exercise correctly, you didn't consciously try to move the pendulum, and you didn't feel the movement.

Your nervous system and your muscular system work together, and as you imagine the movement and visualize it, the muscles in your arm are firing in the same sequence as they would if you were consciously moving the pendulum. Your hand and arm are not moving enough to be seen or felt, but the length of the pendulum string magnifies the movement so it can be seen.

Now let's apply this principle to baseball. What would you do if a coach told you to practice throwing hanging curveballs or throwing your fastball in the dirt during your bullpen? How about if he asked you to swing at pitches in the dirt during BP? You wouldn't do it, right? No, because it wouldn't make sense to practice skills in a negative way.

The same principle applies if you go back to the hotel or your apartment after the game and lie in bed visualizing the hanging curveball you threw or the swing you took at the pitch out of the strike zone, for the last out. You are actually practicing that "skill" — the wrong skill — all over again.

Then, the next time you find yourself in a similar situation, you are more likely to fail in exactly the same way since you have been practicing failure both mentally (self-concept) and physically (neuromuscular). This visualization is just as powerful as practicing on the field. In fact, it is more powerful. When you imagine failure, your self-concept takes a hit, and so does your neuromuscular system. Success breeds success, and failure breeds failure. Practice success!

Two New Thought Patterns to Increase Success

As indicated earlier, you need to get out of your current comfort zone if you want to play at a higher level, and that means you must change the way you think. Reexamine two thoughts: your current definitions of the terms "change" and "winning."

Redefine Change and Embrace It

If you're not completely happy with the results you've had to date, you need to change. It's been said, "If you keep doing what you've always done, you'll keep getting what you've always gotten." Einstein said it somewhat differently. He stated, "The definition of insanity is to continue to do things the same way and expect different results."

It's human nature to resist change. You've established a pattern of thinking and behaving that's comfortable, so being confronted with change automatically creates stress and resistance. You have to leave your comfort zone if you want to grow.

Resistance can take many forms. For example resisting change in your physical game might manifest as "arguing for your limitations." When you've introduced new ideas or changes in your swing or your delivery, you've probably heard that little voice in the back of your head whispering, "It doesn't feel right," "It's not comfortable," "This won't work for me," or "I'm playing well now so why should I change?" Of course something new won't "feel right" when you initially try it. The old way has become a habit. It's so ingrained in your neuromuscular system that it's automatic — but that doesn't mean it's a good habit, nor does it mean you can't change the habit.

To illustrate this point, fold your hands and look at which thumb is on top. Now, shake your hands 10 times, counting all 10 shakes, and fold them quickly again. Chances are the same thumb is on top because folding your hands has become automatic — a habit.

Now let's override that habit. Shake your hands 10 times, again counting all 10 shakes. Immediately fold your hands with the opposite thumb on top. That probably required some thinking — some extra effort on your part. Without thinking — when we're on autopilot — we always revert to our habitual or automatic way of doing things because it feels comfortable. If we make a conscious decision to change, and work at the change, the new way eventually becomes automatic and replaces the old.

The same resistance to change holds true for your mental game. You've become accustomed to thinking a certain way. It's habitual, it's comfortable — but some of it is limiting. You'll need to work to overcome this impulse to fall back into old thinking patterns if you want to improve. The best way to do that is to redefine change in your mind and to make a mental connection between the ideas of change and growth and improved performance. Growth always requires positive change.

Redefine Winning

The second term you need to examine is winning. As a former athlete and coach myself, I know that the ultimate goal of any competition is to come out on top. But if you're concentrating on beating your opponent, your focus is in the wrong place. Every time you lose, you are a failure in your own mind — regardless of how well you played. And once again, your self-image takes a beating.

It is precisely this type of thinking you need to adjust if you want to consistently play at your best. Looking at winning from a different perspective will require you to step out of your current comfort zone.

In 1987 I published a book titled *Coaching the Mindset for Winning*. I discussed winning and the importance of reframing the prevalent belief that winning is always defeating an opponent. In that book I defined winning as:

- Establishing a goal and doing everything necessary (physically and mentally) to move confidently toward that goal.

- Developing your God-given talents to the maximum.

- Utilizing every resource available to develop these talents.

- Entering each game expecting, not hoping, to do well.

- Doing your best, not necessarily being the best.

> *The opponent is not the enemy. They're our partner in the dance.*
>
> PHIL JACKSON

When you practice this concept of winning, you not only enjoy the competitive experience more, but you actually begin to come out on top more often. You have stopped defeating yourself. Once you get out of your own way, you'll find the sky is the limit because you can now play without restrictions. When you play with this mindset, you often find yourself lost in the moment, just playing the game — and having fun again.

In this mindset, you play with complete abandon, complete freedom and complete focus. When lost in the moment, you play with no inhibition, no embarrassment, and no concern for what others might think. You trust your ability, and things just seem to fall into place. When you play to be the best you can be, you can walk away proud

of your effort because it was a total effort. The winni
about beating someone else. It's about being the best
be, each and every day.

As this new view of winning takes hold, you will perform more consistently because you will be able to play unencumbered by concerns for the outcome, and you will remain on an even keel emotionally. Essentially, your view will change so that you will:

- See where you could be, not where you are.

- See what you want to happen, not what you want to avoid.

- Expect to win, not hope to win!

If you want to play up to your potential, you will work to develop this mindset and take ownership of your thoughts. When you do, you will find yourself winning by the old definition more often than you ever did in the past.

In Sum...

- Making minor changes in your thinking and behaviors can have a major impact on improving your performance.

- Most players, regardless of their success, fall short of reaching their full potential; they've developed a false ceiling that limits their performance.

- To remove this false ceiling and reach your potential, you need a comprehensive approach — working on both your physical skills as well as your mental approach.

- The proper mental approach benefits you in two ways. First, it increases your self-image cycle, which improves your confidence level, and second, it helps create and reinforce the proper muscle memory needed for consistent performance.

- You need to redefine winning. Winning means being and playing at the very best you can be today — both physically and mentally. It doesn't always means being your best. It means being the best you can be today.

- You need to be open to and comfortable with change because positive growth occurs only when you create positive change in your habits. Habits and thoughts can be changed if you are committed to improvement.

CHAPTER 3

Limiting Performance

*"Our deepest fear is not that we are inadequate.
Our deepest fear is that we are powerful beyond
measure. It is our light, not our darkness,
that most frightens us."*

Marianne Williamson, Author

If you have ever struggled to improve your performance, chances are you have become familiar with the feeling that there's a lid on your game. That feeling may well be true. You may have limited your performance — without even realizing it — by establishing that false or invisible ceiling discussed in the previous chapter. The following example is based on a position player I worked with, but it can be applied to all players — pitchers and position players alike. This discussion will cover several principles that create this ceiling and how these principles can be repurposed to destroy your false beliefs and propel your performance to a whole new level. These are natural principles at work, and — like gravity — they always work. You just need to learn how they work so you can make them work for you instead of against you.

One Player's Story

Over the years, a player develops a belief (self-concept) about his ability to hit. For example, in his mind, he sees himself as a .270 to .280 hitter. (If you're a pitcher, reframe this example with a pitching statistic such as ERA, BB per 9 innings, etc.) When he's playing at or near that level, things are going well. He is confident, playing consistently, relaxed, and having fun — he's performing in his comfort zone (CZ). The level just above this range is his false ceiling. He has more potential than he's displaying on the field, but he's become comfortable within this range and he gets by.

He may be playing well, but he's not playing up to his potential. He's playing up to his belief level. Remember, you don't perform up to your potential; you perform up to your belief. As we reviewed in Chapter 2, you can't out-perform your self-image.

For several years this player hit at or near that range. But what would happen if he starts the year hot and a month or two into the season, he's hitting .320, maybe .330, or even .400? He's gotten out of his CZ of .270 to .280, and it doesn't fit his inner image of his identity. Since the body is a self-regulating mechanism, he needs to self-regulate — to get back to "who he really is." So he comes up with creative ways to get back *down* to where he's comfortable.

He may fall prey to the perceived stress of having to continue to carry the team, or maybe he sabotages his routine, has trouble sleeping, gives up his mental training or feels uncomfortable fielding questions from reporters. It could be a simple change in his thinking such as, "I know this can't last, so I'd better enjoy it while I can." In any case, over the next month or two, his stress level (not at the conscious level, but the subconscious level) slowly begins to climb, and his subconscious mind finds creative ways to change behavior, initiate a slump, and get him back to "normal" — into the .280 range where he thinks he belongs. As he approaches this level, the stress slowly decreases, and he returns to his "consistent self" again.

Now let's imagine the same player starts the year cold, and he's hitting .200. Again, he's out of his CZ, but this time he's below it, and he feels the stress. In this situation his subconscious mind becomes creative in finding ways to get back up into his comfort zone. He may become more focused or goal oriented, get more sleep, or even begin to do mental training. He may go back to a routine that worked for him in the past. In any case, he will change his behaviors — just enough to get him back to his image of "who he really is." These behaviors heat up his performance for several weeks. As his average approaches the .270 to .280 range, the stress lessens. He becomes his normal, consistent self again. He no longer has to stay hot, and he lets the false ceiling set in again.

Beliefs versus Truths

Remember what we said about truth? There's my truth, your truth and the truth. But beliefs are not necessarily the truth. They are only the truth as you see it. Anytime you get too far out of your CZ — either too far above it or too far below it — you'll feel stressed, and your mind and body will automatically self-regulate. The mind-body connection will do whatever is necessary to get you back to where it feels most comfortable.

This scenario plays out with power numbers — OBP, BA, SB, ERA, BB per 9 innings — you name it. It happens over and over again in baseball. Some players believe they always start the year off hot and that they cool down in June, July or August. Others start the year off cold and heat up with the weather.

Some pitchers believe they tire after 100 pitches because they've been conditioned to believe it. Others *know* they struggle in the first inning or maybe in the fourth. Some players don't have good self-discipline, while others are always pushing the rules to the limit. Maybe some can't lay down a bunt to save their lives, and others can't maintain their patience at the plate. And no matter what they believe, *they are right!* Their beliefs become a self-fulfilling prophecy.

You've seen teammates and other players go through similar scenarios, and at times it's happened to you. We all revert to our comfort zone when we're under stress, which explains why it is so difficult to take new skills into a game, where the tension level is so much higher than in batting practice or the bullpen.

Imagine the trajectory your career would take if you alter these inner beliefs (your self-concept), reset your comfort zone at a higher level, and smash through that false ceiling and its self-fulfilling prophecies. The great news is you *can* and *will* if you decide to! The process is quite simple, and it begins with an understanding of how this limited thinking was established in the first place. With that knowledge, you can use the same principles to help you reset thinking at a higher level. First, let's look at how fear of both success and failure keeps you in your comfort zone.

Fear and the Comfort Zone (CZ)

Both fear of failure and fear of success play a role in keeping your performance safely within your CZ. As illustrated by the example at the beginning of this chapter, anytime you play above or below your CZ, your subconscious will believe your self-image is at stake and will create stress, and you'll unwittingly get creative with ways to get you back to who you believe you are, your self-image.

In working with hundreds of professional players over the years, I have found that for those playing below their CZs, the fear of failure generates a feeling of desperation — a form of stress that motivates them to get back to playing at their belief level/their CZ. Even players who shy away from the mental game are willing to try anything, even working on their "mental game," because of this emotional feeling of desperation.

I've also found that when players play above their CZ, it's the fear of success that creates the stress that then negatively affects performance. If a player is "too successful" he may encounter additional stressors such as increased media scrutiny, increased public recognition, a contract he feels obligated to "live up to," etc. There may be an inner fear of these additional stressors at the subconscious level that needs to be identified and overcome to reach your potential.

Nelson Mandela quoted Marianne Williamson in his 1994 inauguration speech as president of South Africa. In that address he stated, "Our deepest fear is not that we are inadequate. Our deepest fear is that we are powerful beyond measure. It is our light, not our darkness,

that most frightens us. We ask ourselves, who am I to be brillia..
geous, talented and fabulous?" He then went on to answer that que.
tion. "Actually, who are you not to be? You are a child of God. Your
playing small doesn't serve the world."

To reset your CZ to a higher level, you have to overcome these
fears because their motivation is only temporary. Countless times I've
worked with players who struggle, get motivated by their fear of failure, then get hot and play at an extremely high level for weeks. As
soon as they get back into their CZ and approach the upper level,
the feeling of desperation that originally motivated them disappears
and they settle in. You must find a deeper inspiration to maintain your
motivation.

Desperation kicks in and motivates you when playing below
your comfort zone. To keep playing well and to break out of your
comfort zone on the topside, you need a dose of inspiration.

There are plenty of clichés about success, such as "The road to
success is always under construction," and "The road to success is lined
with many tempting parking spaces." That's why the comfort zone is
so dangerous — it's a place for rest when what you need most is to
keep moving and break out on the topside.

To reset your CZ at a higher level, you need to reset your self-
image at a higher level. You need to get comfortable at a higher performance level. Now that you have a better understanding of how
fear can sabotage your performance, we'll look at the simple process
of breaking through the ceiling. It all starts with understanding how
that ceiling got built in the first place.

The Power of Imagination

Your body cannot tell the difference between a real experience
and an imagined experience. Anytime you vividly imagine something,
your body reacts as if it is going through that experience. This principle explains why imagery is so powerful. When you visualize, chemical changes can occur, your self-image can be altered, neuromuscular

patterns can be reinforced or altered — and all three of these can have positive or negative effects, depending on what you visualize.

A simple example illustrates this principle from the chemical standpoint. Have you ever lain in bed and thought of a stressful situation, then found you were unable to sleep? Maybe it was revisiting something that occurred in the past, such as an argument, striking out in a key situation, or walking someone with the bases loaded. Perhaps it was projecting negative thoughts into the future, like worrying about tomorrow's game or a talk you have to give to a youth group.

If the images are vivid and your thoughts are stressful, chemicals are released that set off your stress response, which prevents sleep. Your body has accepted as real these imagined experiences as real ones, and it has responded with real reactions.

You Are What You Tell Yourself and Imagine Yourself to Be

Who you are today as a player is a result of your previous self-talk and the images you held in your mind yesterday, last week and last year. And the person and player you will be tomorrow will be a result of your self-talk and the images you hold in your mind today. You can't control yesterday because it's past and gone, nor can you control tomorrow — that's the future and the unknown. The only thing you can control is what's occurring today, right now. Take control and remember that although you can't control the future, you can influence it with your current thoughts, self-talk and visualizations.

In Sum...

- You perform at the level of your self-image, not your potential.
- You always self-regulate to return to your inner-belief level.
- Your comfort zone determines your success zone (CZ = SZ).
- To reset your comfort zone, you must change your self-image.
- Your body can't tell the difference between a real and an imagined experience.
- Your self-talk and the images you hold in your mind determine your behaviors.

CHAPTER 4

Your Powerful Mind

"You are today where your thoughts have brought you; you will be tomorrow where your thoughts take you."

James Allen

I was listening to MLB on Sirius/XM radio and heard an advertisement for the Rosetta Stone language program. The ad stated, "You'll learn your new language just like you learned your first language, and you'll begin to speak the new language in 10 minutes." We'll take the same approach to resetting your comfort zone at a higher level — the approach you used to set it in the first place. And, like the Rosetta Stone program, in 10 minutes you'll begin to speak this new language. You won't be fluent in 10 minutes, but you will begin to learn these new habits.

Your Mind

Since resetting your comfort zone uses the same process you used to establish it in the first place, it only makes sense that you'll need to understand the process of creating it in more detail. Of course this explanation will be an oversimplification of the intricate process of how your mind works. The examples and figures I present are not scientifically accurate, but they do illustrate key points that give you a better understanding of how your subconscious beliefs were developed and how your mind influences and dictates your performance on the field.

Your mind is composed of many different parts, and each has a unique function. To keep things simple, we will focus on only three parts: your conscious mind (CM), your subconscious mind (SM) and the reticular activating system (RAS).

The Conscious Mind (CM)

The conscious mind is the part that you are aware of during the day. It's where you do your thinking and reasoning and where you make decisions and exercise your free will. It is fairly limited in what it can do on its own, but it plays a major role because it directs or tells the subconscious mind what it needs to do. Think of your conscious mind as the boss — the general, the goal setter.

The Subconscious Mind (SM)

Your subconscious mind is also referred to as the non-conscious as well as the un-conscious mind. We'll use the term subconscious throughout to represent all of these terms.

Your subconscious makes up the major portion of your brain mass, and it is not only the largest part of your mind, but the most powerful. It can process millions of bits of information per second. It contains all past memories, your intelligence and your wisdom. It also runs your body, so to speak, by keeping your heart beating, controlling your digestion, regulating your breathing, etc.

Think of your subconscious mind as being a "goal seeker." It does exactly what it is told to do. It is designed to find every means possible to help you accomplish goals the conscious mind has set. It does this in a variety of ways — the subconscious is the source of creativity. It recognizes factors in your environment that you normally wouldn't notice but that will assist you toward your goals, and it "tells you" what behaviors to engage in to accomplish your goals.

Your subconscious mind *does not evaluate* what the conscious mind tells it to do, it simply accepts the task and does it. Whether the task has a positive or negative affect on your performance is not a consideration.

One way to link the conscious and subconscious is to think of your mind as a garden. The conscious mind is the gardener — the boss who does the planting. The subconscious mind is the soil. The soil is fertile and will grow whatever is planted and nurtured by the gardener. The seeds are the conscious thoughts. You fertilize and water these seeds with your self-talk — your inner chatter and images you form in your mind.

As the gardener, you are planting seeds all day long, often without being aware of it. Many times the seeds we plant are weeds — negative thoughts you planted by mistake. Each time you think similar negative thoughts, you are watering these unwanted negative seeds and assisting them to grow. The same holds true for the plants you do want to grow.

Whatever you plant (your thoughts) and cultivate (your self-talk and imagery) in your subconscious mind will grow, and you display the results in your behaviors and your performance. Since you are the gardener, it's important that you make sure you are planting and cultivating positive seeds.

Reticular Activating System (RAS)

The third part of the mind important for our purposes is the reticular activating system, which we'll refer to as the RAS. Throughout the day you are exposed to thousands of stimuli, and you would literally go crazy if you were aware of it all. To keep you from becoming overwhelmed by all this information, the RAS acts as a filter. It filters out unimportant stimuli and allows only information that's important to you to get through.

Think of the RAS as a guard at the doorway of your mind, allowing in only approved information. Its function is to sort through the myriad of stimuli and look for information you programmed in as important. If something meets your criteria, it is allowed to pass through this filter to your subconscious, which then goes to work as a goal seeker.

A great example of how the RAS works is explained in the book *The Answer*. The authors, Assaraf and Smith, use Google as a metaphor for the RAS. When you type a search on Google:

> "It scours the Internet for everything it can find that relates to the specific phrase, then retrieves it and presents it to you for inspection, and it does this in a matter of seconds. Your reticular formation does much the same thing, only it does its work not in seconds but in thousandths of a second."

Just like doing a search on Google, Yahoo or any other search engine, you enter the information you want to search for according to your goals — default or others — whatever you consider important, and the RAS works 24/7, searching for whatever you told it to find.

The following are examples of the RAS at work. Let's say that you never had any interest in cars. You never notice them even though you see countless numbers of them each year. Because you had no interest in cars to date, your RAS filtered out thoughts about cars because you didn't consider them important. Then one day you decide to buy a car. Almost immediately you begin noticing various models as you drive to work, and you begin to notice ads on TV. You even see cars for sale on the side of the road that you never before noticed.

When you decide upon a particular car model and purchase it, you start noticing that car model on the highway without consciously looking for it. Since your subconscious "sees all," it brings these cars to your conscious awareness because you have identified cars as important. This is your subconscious confirming your purchase. You may even notice not only the same model, but also the same year and even color.

I was using the above example of how the RAS works with a major league shortstop when he broke into a broad smile and gave me a perfect example he'd recently noticed. He said he never noticed pregnant women until the previous month, when he learned his wife was pregnant. "Now pregnant women are all over the place — you wouldn't believe how many there are!"

Cars and pregnant women are always to be found, but neither noticed until they became objects of interest. Only then could they penetrate the RAS filter.

Figure 4-1 illustrates how these three parts of your mind work together. Think of the conscious and subconscious mind as a gear system. In this system, the smaller of the two, the conscious mind, powers the subconscious mind. Goals that penetrate the RAS are the fuel that activates this gear system to get the subconscious moving.

FIGURE 4-1

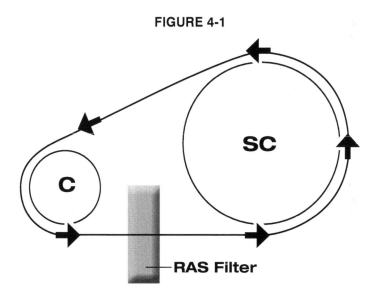

Neuroplasticity

One of the greatest discoveries made by neuroscientists over the past 15 years is called *neuroplasticity*. For many years it was thought that brain circuitry, once established, set the tone for life. That during childhood and early adolescence, the brain became hardwired and this pretty much determined how we view the world and experiences in life.

The discovery of *neuroplasticity* changed that thinking. It is now known that no matter what your age, your brain is capable of creating entirely new neural pathways. Your brain can be rewired based on the information it receives. Your dominant thoughts systematically reinforce new pathways that alter your way of thinking and thus your habits and behaviors. Powering this system are goals.

Goals Power Change

It's the goals you set, either consciously or through default, that pass through the RAS and get the gears moving, so let's take a look at those goals.

Consciously Set Goals

Some goals take shape when you purposely set them as desired accomplishments. Once you decide what you want to achieve, you systematically impress those goals on your subconscious through a variety of methods: by reflecting on them, through your self-talk (affirmations) or through visualizing them (either by planning to do so or through day dreaming). Once these goals pass through the RAS, your subconscious mind takes over. As a goal seeker, your subconscious searches for things in your environment that will help you achieve your desired results.

Default Goals

The second way that goals get through the RAS and activate your subconscious is through default. Default goals are established when you spend considerable time reflecting or thinking about something, letting your self-talk chatter on about something, and visualizing something without really choosing to do so. In other words, you don't consciously choose to send these goals forward. They become goals because they have become your dominant thought pattern. Default goals are established when you repeatedly send similar thoughts to your subconscious that are not analyzed, not thought out and not properly evaluated.

Most default goals are limiting because you don't consciously set them. Although you may think that bad things "just happen," they actually follow the same pattern as consciously set goals. The problem is that you are systematically imprinting the wrong goals into your subconscious, and that sets it working to meet these negative goals.

Listed below are examples of how negative and self-limiting behaviors can be established through default.

1. You get frustrated and set default goals through negative self-talk such as "I'm horse shit," "I suck," "I'm Mr. Joe Average," "It's out of my control," etc. These are all comments I've heard from players. Now, the subconscious mind takes on its task to find creative ways to prove you are "right" and bring these thoughts to reality.

2. You accept what others say about you as being true without evaluating properly. A parent may have said something such as "You'll never amount to anything" years ago. They may have said it to motivate you, but instead of being motivated, you accepted it as true. Another example would be overhearing a coach tell someone, "He can't throw worth a darn," and because the coach is respected in baseball circles, you accept this as true. Once accepted, these inner beliefs, even though they are false, will affect your performance.

3. You don't properly evaluate your experiences. Say you've had several days where you had quality at bats but lined out or had several outstanding defensive plays take away possible hits. You begin to think, "I can't buy a hit." Sure enough, once again, you're right! And thus begins an extended slump. Remember, your thinking becomes a self-fulfilling prophecy!

It's the default goals that get you in the long run. They establish false and limiting boundaries on your self-concept, and they can keep you in your comfort zone or take you below your comfort zone into a slump, limiting your performance. In the examples above, the goals were set because of poor evaluation of the data and by not monitoring and controlling the accompanying thoughts and self-talk.

Most attitudes, beliefs, behaviors and expectations — all of which drive your performance — were acquired through your self-talk, the words you use when you talk to yourself. It's this inner chatter, the conversations you carry on with yourself — in the car, in bed at night when you can't sleep, while working out, when on the mound or in the on-deck circle — that accumulate and establish your belief system, your self-concept, and thus set your comfort zone and your success zone.

And remember, thoughts don't just evaporate — they are recorded in the neurons of your brain. These are the seeds your subconscious accepts and grows, especially when you tend to them repetitively — when you tell yourself, "I'm horse shit at this," "I can't buy a break," "He's really throwing smoke." Or you may ask a question such as, "Why do I suck so bad?" The problem with the question is that you answer it. It doesn't have to be the truth, it only has to be the truth as you see it.

Your Brain as a Computer

Now let's look at what happens when you send limiting thoughts to your brain. You've heard the comparisons between your brain and a computer. Again, the comparison of the two is an over-simplification, but this comparison will help clarify how to reset your success zone at a higher level.

Think of your brain as your internal computer where you have stored all of the information from your life. Everything you have ever heard, seen or experienced is etched on the hard drive of your subconscious. All of your beliefs, attitudes, habits and behaviors reside in this internal hard drive. Remember that the information stored there is *not necessarily the truth; it is only the truth as you've entered it.*

What information is stored on your hard drive? Is it really the truth? Is it helping you meet your goals, or is it hindering your success? Let's look at what happens if the information is *not* the real truth.

The GIGO Principle

Computer geeks often speak of the GIGO principle. GIGO is an acronym for "Garbage in, garbage out." If you turn on your computer, open a document and type 3 + 3 = 2 and press the print key, you get 3 + 3 = 2 printed out on paper. Obviously this is not the correct answer so you type it in again — 3 + 3 = 2 — and press the print key. Once again you get a printout that is incorrect.

No matter how many times you type in incorrect information, you'll always get the wrong result when you hit print — *period*. It doesn't matter how determined or persistent you are or how much you desire to get it right. If you input the wrong data, you will always get the wrong result. Your brain is much like this computer. The *only* way to alter the end result is to change the input.

To Grow Your Success Zone, You Must Change

You have created a world of "facts" that you believe to be true, and you live the life and play the game of baseball according to these "facts." They determine how you act, behave, and respond. They determine your attitudes, your beliefs, your habits, behaviors, expectations and ultimately how successful you will be. They set the boundaries for your success zone. As we've learned, many of these "facts" are *not* really true. But if you believe them to be true, you behave accordingly, and they prevent you from performing at your best. They literally prevent you from releasing all of your internal horsepower (potential).

If you continue to put these false facts into your computer, you'll continue to get the same results — it's the GIGO principle of life. The question becomes how you can change these facts and reset them at a higher level — at a true level. The answer is to reboot the computer and change the input so you're working with new, well-planned, more-accurate data.

The process is simple, and it uses the same principles that set the boundaries for you in the first place — except now you will control the input. No more default goals! In Parts 2 and 3 we'll go over the information you need to make these changes.

In Sum...

- To grow you must change. Without change there can be no growth.
- Your brain operates like a computer. Input = Output.
- You need to control the input so that it matches your goals.
- You use your conscious mind to identify the proper input.
- When you impress this input on your subconscious mind in a systematic way, change can occur quickly and permanently.

PART 2
Laying the Foundation for Change

The purpose of Part 2 is to identify the changes you need to make to take your performance to a higher level. As discussed earlier, the majority of your behaviors (both physical and mental) are correct, and they got you where you are. It's that small 2 to 5 percent of your thinking that needs to be addressed.

The opening chapter of Part 2 will illustrate how the evaluation process can help you identify behaviors and thought patterns that have limited you in the past. Once you identify behaviors that hold you back, you'll be able to focus your efforts on them, and then, through goal setting (Chapter 6), you'll consciously begin to reset your RAS to move you toward these new behaviors.

Both your conscious and your subconscious mind are tools in the change process. Part 2 focuses on using your conscious mind. During the evaluation process, you'll use it to identify thoughts, attitudes, behaviors and habits that have hindered your performance. Next, you'll use your conscious mind again in the goal-setting process to identify the new behaviors you need to exhibit to move from where you are now to where you want to go in the future.

CHAPTER 5

The Evaluation Process

"It's Not the Arrow, It's the Indian"

Unknown

I was sitting in the dugout talking with a Triple A player with the Tacoma Rainiers discussing the mental game and the importance of taking responsibility for one's actions. He summarized our discussion by saying, "You mean, it's not the arrow, it's the Indian." Yep, he nailed it on the head.

Many players look outside of themselves for answers that can be found only by looking within. They blame coaches, umpires, the weather, bad luck or a poor defense. They find some excuse for poor performance rather than looking within themselves. Their pride may actually prevent them from meeting their goals without them even being aware of it. When a player reverts to this line of reasoning, I immediately stop him and point out that if things are beyond his control, he can't change them. He can only change those things he controls, so let's focus on those.

It's only logical to take complete responsibility for all aspects of your performance. The starting point is this inner reflection called evaluation. Step 1 of the 6th Tool program is to look in the mirror to identify your current "inner blueprint." Identify the beliefs, thought patterns and habits that are holding you back.

The Evaluation Process

When I meet with players individually, one of the vital roles I play is to help each player carry out a detailed self-evaluation and assist him by providing a different perspective than that offered by coaches, family, friends or even themselves — their personal perspective. Players often view themselves in a much different light than how others see them.

You need a clear picture of the "true you." The only way to get this is through a comprehensive self-examination as well as an evaluation from others.

Remember the GIGO principle from Chapter 4, "Garbage in, garbage out"? The same is true of your self-analysis. If you are less than honest with yourself in this evaluation process, you'll end up with false information. The self-examination step is important because, when done correctly, it forces you to honestly identify your weaknesses, parts of your game and thought patterns that may be holding you back. You may find that your mental preparation, or lack thereof, might just be one reason you aren't playing at your best.

I've found that when players struggle, they are more eager to talk about how they are working on their mechanics, taking extra time in the cages or in the bullpen working with coaches. They spend countless hours on special drills and extra work. Some even change their diet, shave their heads, or, as the Yankees' Jason Giambi did, wear golden-colored "thongs" under his uniform to change his luck. Most players would do anything to change their "luck" — anything, that is, but admit they need to work on their thinking, their mental game.

During the evaluation process you will need to be brutally honest with yourself so that you can identify any and all of the shortcomings that may be holding you back. If you are too proud to do an honest evaluation and to evaluate your mental approach when searching for weaknesses that need improvement, you'll have to be content with mediocrity. It's never convenient to perform a thorough evaluation; it's usually painful, difficult and often time consuming. It's easier to "argue for your limitations" and cling to the old ways of doing things than it is to change. Remember, if you cling to the old, you'll continue to get the same old results.

Results Reveal the Truth

What type of data has been entered into your inner computer? It's a pretty simple process to find out — just look at your results! The results are the facts. They identify your inner blueprint. It's this inner guidance system that has set your limits thus far, so your results are an excellent barometer to identify what needs to change.

Self-Evaluation

Self-evaluation is the first step in the examination process. Its purpose is not to identify and focus on weaknesses, but to help you grow and become all that you can be. If you want to grow, you first need to evaluate where you are.

You need to ask questions to evaluate, and not just any questions — the right ones. If you ask the wrong questions, you won't get the answers you need. I'll pose some questions to start the process to help you examine your past performances. This will provide you with an idea of the type of questions to ask so that you can identify changes that will be beneficial. You'll notice that once you start asking yourself the right questions and exploring what may be holding you back, your subconscious mind will work on this task 24/7. Once you begin this process, thoughts, ideas and inspirations will appear as if out of nowhere over the next week or two. Pay attention to these hunches or intuitions. Your subconscious may be talking to you. Take the time to listen.

Your Turn

Here are some thoughts on how to begin.

- If you're a position player, look at your batting average, power numbers, on-base percentage, etc. If you're a pitcher, look at your ERA, BB per 9 innings, innings pitched per year, etc. Are they as high or as low as you believe they could be?

Your thoughts here: _No I believe my success rate of delivery* can be higher_

*Delivery: Accurate, Clear, Succinct the Gist to me

- Examine your consistency. Do you consistently play in the upper third of your ability level? Or do you have major ups and downs, sometimes being in the zone and displaying your true ability, and then correcting the "mistake" and drifting back to your comfort zone (CZ). Do you see a pattern here?

Your thoughts here: _No I have ups and downs. even in a day, but certainly over larger time periods_

- Do you struggle at specific times? For example, do you start the year strong (or poorly) and then cool down (or heat up) with the weather? Do you have a poor June, July or fade in August? Maybe it's the 1st inning or maybe it's the 4th or 5th that always causes the problem for you. Can you count on never getting a hit during your first AB? Or do you get a hit early, and then you coast and can't seem to get multi-hit games? Can you see a specific pattern in your performance that has developed over the years?

Your thoughts here: _Seems I consistently start strong and hit a point... looking for the next thing... In reflection I rarely fully complete any thing_

- Examine your dominant thought patterns. For example, if you listed an inability to get multi-hit games, maybe you've had thoughts such as, "I always get a hit early in the game, but can't seem to get the multi-hit game." Or if you are a pitcher and ALWAYS tire after 100 pitches, does your self-talk support this belief? Have you ever thought, "I'm good for 100 pitches, but then I'm tired out." You may not actually physically tire after 100 pitches, but you will tire if that's your belief. The real culprit may be your self-talk, which activates your mind to search for exhaustion as you approach this limit. This is a great example of self-fulfilling prophecy. Your inner dialogue may have set the limit. Is your self-talk positive? Can you identify negative self-talk in any phase of your game that may set self-imposed limits?

Your thoughts here: _I know I can make a first impression (positive) - something w/o speechy... but that quickly is challenged - so can sometimes I repeat to myself don't speak or "you'll erase yourself"; ☺_

- Are there any behaviors that may be counterproductive to your success? Ask yourself questions such as, "Am I a pleaser, always trying to please coaches or others?" "Do I have difficulty following rules or being on time?" "Am I a good teammate?" "Do I have trouble communicating with coaches or teammates?" Or "Do I have trouble following through with commitments I make?"

Your thoughts here: _Always trying to please others. It aggrivates me that others will speak critical of me to "behind my back" to the point I'm always following up to see how others read situations or what I needed._

- Look at your numbers. Have you produced them consistently over time, or have you produced them in spurts?

  Your thoughts here: _Spurts — Annally my revenus have been done over the past 3 years — w/in a year, month, day — performance is sporadic_

- Is there any part of your game where you're not as satisfied as you'd like to be?

  Your thoughts here: _Communication ; Commit — I'm too wisky ущащу - looking for consensus w/ making decision and influency/leading... I don't trust my decision making_

- Do you have written goals or are your goals only in your mind? Research points out that written goals are more powerful than unwritten goals. If not written down, the "goals" you have in your mind are merely dreams or desires, not real goals that stimulate your unconscious mind.

  Your thoughts here: _Written work goals, "In my mind" personal goals_

- Are your goals realistic? Have you set them high enough so they motivate you, or have you set them within your comfort zone so as not to feel pressure? Ask yourself, "Have I set realistic goals, or were they too high or too low?"

Your thoughts here: _Yes I think they are realistic_

- Are you flexible with your goals? As circumstances change, are you open to revisiting and adapting them as needed?

Your thoughts here: _yes_

- As you approach your goals, do you reset them before you accomplish them? Once you near a goal, the tendency is to back off and lose momentum rather than to reset them at a higher level. This is especially true when you've played below your belief, you've gotten hot and are approaching your comfort zone. This prevents you from breaking out on the topside.

Your thoughts here: _All the time - it goes back to my point that I don't think. I find h everything_

- What thoughts, self-talk, or beliefs do you have that may be self-limiting?

Your thoughts here: _"I suck" ; "Just shutup" -_
"I have to get out of here" ...
"Worthless". Doubting I not judge the
best thing for everyone : Family ? work if I
Just vanished

- Have you been told by coaches that you need to correct a behavior or do something differently, yet you believe you are fine just the way you are? Maybe you've heard you're negative, not attacking the strike zone, need to be more selective at the plate, need to be more of a leader, etc. What are some things that coaches have told you in the past that you might have resisted? Revisit them now in your mind.

Your thoughts here: _I've been given feedback_
TANGIBLE DELIVERABLES

- What off-field behaviors may affect your on-field performance? Do you get enough rest at night? Has anyone ever suggested you drink too much? Maybe party too hard? Have poor eating habits? Do you fret about things you can't control? Are you negative in the home setting?

Your thoughts here: _Little Rest ; Don't drink ;_
Good (not great) Eating habit
Fret about things I con't control
Sometimes negative @ home

- What type of people do you hang around with? Are they supportive and heading in the same direction as you are? Do they encourage positive behaviors that will further your career?
Your thoughts here: _Don't hang around_
too many people; in fact none
nearby.

- Have you placed extra stress on yourself because you feel you need to "live up to a contract," or "live up to the hype" that has appeared in the papers? How about stressing because it is a contract year or you have concerns about being traded?
Your thoughts here: _Yes - every day_

The Psychological Development Form

Years ago I developed a short, two-page form for players to use in examining behaviors that are part of their mental game. This form, titled the Psychological Development Form (PDF) is found in Appendix A. It is a quick and easy way to add to your self-evaluation. On this form, you simply grade yourself from low (1) to high (10) on 12 separate categories. It can help you identify behaviors in your mental game that may be worth addressing. A larger copy of this form is available at the website (**www.baseballs6thtool.com**).

Getting Input from Others

Even if you feel you are a good self-evaluator, you may find it beneficial to get input from trusted outside sources. Ask a coach or a teammate you respect to give you an unbiased view of behaviors they believe you could improve as a player.

There are many ways to do this. An easy one may be to have a coach or several coaches fill out the Psychological Development Form from their perspective. You can compare your results to those of each coach. Look for differences that may indicate either your evaluation — or the coaches' — is off. Discuss differences with your coach. This is a great way to delve into more depth and get some needed feedback for consideration.

I was once asked by coaches to talk with a double A pitcher who they felt had some of the worst work habits they'd ever seen in a professional player. I met with the player and gave him the PDF. I did the same with the coaches on the staff. The staff rated his effort/work habits as a 1 on the 10-point scale (1 being poor). The player self-evaluated this same area as a perfect 10 — outstanding! He felt he was the hardest worker on the team. It took a lengthy meeting with the player and the staff to correct the situation. It turned out that the three coaches were correct. The player listened, changed his behavior, and eventually moved on to a big league career.

When getting input from others, be sure it is from people you trust and who will keep things confidential. Also, remember it is just their viewpoint. They may not be accurate in their evaluation, but their thoughts should at least give you needed information to consider as you put together your program for change. As stated earlier, there is "your truth, their truth and the truth." Chances are "the truth" may lie somewhere between the other two.

Who could you approach to get an unbiased view? List names below:

Name: _____

Name: _____

Here's a sample of how you can approach a coach or respected person for input.

"_____, I respect you as both a person and a coach (player), and I'd like to ask you for your unbiased input regarding my behaviors and performance. You've observed me for the past ___ (number of weeks, months or years), and I'd like your opinion as to what I need to work on to improve my game. I'd like you'd to be completely honest with me. I'm not looking for a pat on the back. I'm looking for constructive feedback that will provide me with things I can work on to become a more complete player. I would appreciate it if you would think about it for the next several days, and I'll get back to you for your input. Would you be willing to do so?"

Evaluation as a Continuous Process

When evaluating, brainstorm on paper and jot down all the thoughts that pop into your head. You can adapt, change, or weight the importance of them at a different time. Evaluation is a continuous process if you want to continue to grow and play better. It is not a one-time process. You change, and your needs change, and evaluations must happen repeatedly as you change.

Your Turn

Pull out a pad of paper, begin with the questions posed above, and then come up with additional questions of your own. It is only after you do the evaluation process, asking the right questions and getting honest answers from yourself and others, that you can identify where you are. This honesty provides the basis for identifying what's preventing you from reaching your goals so that you can develop a program

> *The only person who behaves sensibly is my tailor. He makes new measurements every time he sees me.*
>
> GEORGE BERNARD SHAW

to overcome these habits.

You are always in a state of flux, so you have to evaluate on a regular basis to identify the most important current behaviors you need to reinforce, as well as those you need to change. George Bernard Shaw said, "The only person who behaves sensibly is my tailor. He makes new measurements every time he sees me." You need to do the same. Know thyself! Take new measurements on a regular basis to keep growing.

The questions listed here are provided to give you an idea of where to begin the evaluation process. They are not intended to be complete. They simply provide a starting point. Hopefully you will ask yourself additional questions to get a more complete idea of how to improve your game. You need to evaluate your current behaviors to provide a starting point for establishing new goals, which will be discussed in the next chapter.

Since your previous thoughts, words, actions and inactions have placed you where you are today, it is only logical to evaluate and identify behaviors that have contributed to failure in the past so that you can make better choices in the future.

New York Times best-selling author Mathew Kelly discussed the emergence of two sporting legends during the 1990s — Michael Jordan and Tiger Woods — both of whom enjoyed enormous success in their sports. Jordan, as you may know, was actually cut from his basketball team in high school and yet went on to become the greatest player in basketball history. When he was cut, he went on to press his coach for a reason (one form of evaluation — information from others you respect). When told his free throws were part of his weakness, he went on to practice his free throws — making (not taking but making) 500 free throws a day for years until that skill was a strength. In college when he realized his fadeaway jump shot was a weakness, he worked on it until it became one of his greatest assets on the court.

Similarly, in 1997 when Tiger Woods won the Masters by a record number of strokes, weeks later the 21-year-old announced at a press conference he was taking time off to work on his swing. He and his coach explained that they intended to completely deconstruct and reconstruct his swing because they had discovered a flaw, which they believed would not stand up to the pressure of a tight match. With this new swing he went on to dominate his sport for more than 10 years.

Both Jordan and Woods evaluated their performances on a regular basis to identify strengths and weaknesses, and they worked tirelessly to transform their weaknesses into strengths.

They both used the mental game to their advantage. They consistently evaluated, then developed a plan of action, and then implemented that plan.

In Sum...

- The evaluation process is designed to help you identify behaviors you need to alter to play at your best — to be the best you each day.

- When most players struggle, they tend to look at physical or mechanical reasons and work harder. They usually don't consider that it may be their mental game plan — or lack of one — that may be causing or contributing to their struggles.

- Evaluation is quite simple — just look at your results over time. Results don't lie.

- Once you begin the process, your subconscious will work 24/7 to answer the questions you ask of it. Pay attention to any thoughts, hunches, intuitions or inspirations that may crop up during the day.

CHAPTER 6

Goals: Your Blueprint for Success

"A man has to have goals — for a day, for a lifetime — and that was mine, to have people say, 'There goes Ted Williams, the greatest hitter who ever lived.'"

Ted Williams

Humans are the only creatures that have been blessed with the ability to look into the future. We are able to project into the future and imagine a time that is better than today — and we also have the ability to return to the present and work on making that imagined future a reality.

A powerful way to use this blessing is through the process of goal-setting. Goals not only will allow you to project into the future, but researchers have found that those who utilize goals properly — write them down, commit to them, and develop actions steps based on these goals — are more successful than those who just think about their goals.

Goals allow you to write the script for your future, and they serve a variety of useful functions. They allow you to focus so you know where to concentrate your energy. They serve to motivate you to action. And accomplishing a goal, no matter how small, builds your self-confidence. Although statistics may vary, research studies have found that you can actually improve your chances for achieving the things you want from 30 percent to 50 percent if you focus on your goals. It only makes sense to utilize them to gain this edge.

Best-selling author Max Lucado illustrates the importance of focusing on your goals when he tells the story of a group of climbers scaling a large mountain. The view of the snowcapped peak was absolutely breathtaking. On clear days, when their goal was visible and they could see the peak clearly, the climbers made their greatest progress. They walked briskly, not only energized personally, but climbing as a team, united in complete cooperation as they focused on the summit. At times their route leveled off as they moved sideways, and sometimes their route even went downward, but with their eyes focused on the summit, they knew that each step took them closer to their goal.

Things were drastically different on days when the summit was hidden by clouds. When the drab gray ceiling blocked the sight of their goal, their enthusiasm waned, and the climb became much more difficult as they cast their thoughts inward. With the goal out of sight and their eyes focused on the ground beneath them, they struggled up the mountain with short tempers and cloaked in weariness.

Climbing a mountain is a good metaphor for baseball. The journey to the major leagues is a long one. In fact, the baseball season is long and often compared to a marathon rather than a sprint. A baseball player must keep motivated, day in and day out, throughout the season to be successful. It's easy during those "dog days of summer" to lose much of your enthusiasm. Much like those mountain climbers, you need to keep your goal(s) firmly in sight to maintain your focus and enthusiasm. You need clear, specific and powerful goals to help you overcome the obstacles and challenges you'll meet during the season, as well as during your career.

Anytime you lose sight of your goal or your vision, your motivation

> *Obstacles are what you see when you take your eye off the goal.*
>
> JIM LEFEBVRE

and inspiration can drop off. Instead of seeing an obstacle as an opportunity or challenge and confronting it enthusiastically, each hurdle becomes a roadblock to success. Keeping your goals in sight is critical to maximizing your performance. Your goals trigger your unconscious mind into action, which activates your creative juices and your success mechanism.

Goals and Success

It is estimated that of all players drafted, only 6 to 12 percent ever actually play a game in the major leagues, depending on the organization and the year of the draft. I recently met with an organization's minor league teams, and 50 percent of the players had not been there the previous year. With the odds so low, it is necessary to do everything you can to achieve your baseball dream. Goals, if written and used correctly, can increase your odds for success. They are an important part of a mental game plan.

For you to be successful, you should choose your goals and write them in such a way as to provide the spark you need to come to the park each day confident, full of energy and with a plan for the day. Goals are the pictures of the future you create in your mind. The more often you affirm these goals and visualize yourself accomplishing them, the more your subconscious mind begins to accept these pictures as being true. (Remember from Chapter 3, "Your mind can't tell the difference between a real and an imagined experience.") Since your subconscious accepts these new images as true, it believes you truly are performing at this higher level.

In Chapter 3 we discussed the stress that occurs whenever you perform outside of your CZ. This happens both when playing below or above your current CZ. Using goals properly — along with the affirmation and visualization process — takes you out of your CZ to the topside. When this takes place, stress occurs in your mind, and one of two things must happen to remove this stress.

1. You revert to old behaviors to get you back to your old CZ (this is what has happened in the past to create the false ceiling).

2. Your performance must change for the better to alleviate this stress.

If you do nothing, you will revert to your old habits, and you move back into the old CZ. However, if you choose to continue imprinting this new image in your mind, and it becomes the dominant picture. Your subconscious looks for creative ways to change the old behaviors and remove stress by taking your performance to this higher level. This imprinting begins with goals.

Types of Goals

There are actually four types of goals that activate your subconscious mind and motivate you to action. They are (1) ultimate goals, (2) outcome goals, (3) performance goals and (4) default goals. The first three are ones you consciously set and ones that propel you in the proper direction. The last type, default goals, are not set consciously and will hinder your success on the field.

Ultimate Goals

Jason Selk, in his book 10-Minute Toughness: The Mental-Training Program for Winning Before the Game Begins, describes ultimate goals as the long-range goals you want to accomplish. To establish ultimate goals, you would look into your future and imagine what accomplishments you would like to achieve over your career. Imagine what you'd want the guests at your retirement party to be recalling. Examples would include how you played the game, how you conducted yourself, the type of team player you were and major achievements during your career.

Other examples of ultimate goals may include such things as a batting championship, Cy Young Award, making the All-Star Team, having a 10-year career or, for some players, just making the major leagues. For others it may be to dominate at the major league level. They are your goals — not someone else's. Aim high! Too many players set their ultimate goals too low.

Outcome Goals

Outcome goals are result-oriented and are often called product goals. In the sport of baseball, success is measured in outcome goals. Statistics are available for every conceivable category (and even some that are inconceivable). Outcome goals are used to analyze and compare players and their performance levels.

These goals are measurable and are most effective when they focus on what you want to achieve over the next 12 months or over the season. Examples of outcome goals would be:

- to hit for an average of .290.
- to hit 20 home runs during the season.
- to have a K:BB ratio of 4:1 or 3:1.
- to pitch 150 innings, etc.

Most players focus on outcome goals because they measure your success against others. These goals are the most commonly used in baseball, and while they can be motivating for the most part, they do have weaknesses — the biggest being that outcome goals are usually out of your control. You could perform great and yet the "numbers" wouldn't show it.

Some players who use outcome goals as their primary goal source tend to "scoreboard gaze" during games when they're struggling. This causes their focus to wander from the task at hand. In addition, their stress levels tend to rise at inopportune times. Outcome goals can be powerful if they motivate you to work hard and stay on task. However, outcome goals are not good for everyone and thus need to be used wisely.

Process Goals

Process goals, like outcome goals, are measurable, but the focus is on the action or behavior you are seeking — something that is under your control. Process goals can be used in conjunction with outcome goals or on their own. Process goals can remove the stress that outcome goals cause by placing the focus on the process or action you need to take rather than on the result. What I like about process goals is that they are under your control. But again, they need to be a motivational force to be effective.

Examples of process goals would be improving the percentage of quality at bats from 40 percent to 60 percent, taking 25 ground balls to your left each day, throwing 10 change-ups during your next bullpen, throwing 5 change-ups during your next outing, etc. Note that you are focusing on aspects of the game you can control, not the results, which are out of your control.

To be effective, process goals need to motivate you to action, and they must be measurable. A goal such as "being mentally prepared" would not be measurable, if written in that form. Changing the wording to "Being mentally prepared by completing two 5-minute relaxation sessions each day," would give you a measurable action. Process goals still motivate, but they allow many players to be more relaxed during a game by not focusing on their statistics (which relates more closely to the concept of "winning" discussed in Chapter 2).

Default Goals: Danger Ahead!

Default goals are set randomly and without conscious thought. They can negate all of your hard work and quickly derail your success. If you don't have concrete goals, your dominant thoughts — those thoughts that you allow to occupy your mind, those you dwell on — become goals by default.

Since default goals are not deliberately set, they are, unfortunately, most often negative. And when you unconsciously set negative

default goals, you are setting goals to fail! These goals are pow.
but in a negative way.

Anytime you dwell on fear, worry, negative self-talk, problems,
things you want to avoid, they become your dominant thoughts. In
addition, you input default goals with the books you read, the music
you listen to, conversations you have, etc. You have to be aware of
things you celebrate and spend your time focusing on because they
can become dominant thoughts and default goals. Your RAS filter allows repetitive thoughts through to your subconscious mind, which
then acts on these thoughts. Your subconscious, being a goal-seeking
machine, will do everything in its power to achieve these default goals
just like it does for the outcome and process goals. They will influence
your future behavior.

I've worked with many players whose performances are defined
by default goals, which are major sources of failures and struggles in
baseball. The list of default goals would be unlimited, but examples
of how they play out include poor
plate discipline, behavioral issues, fear
of a pick-off move, throwing problems
or nibbling at the K zone. You don't
consciously set the goal to fail, but you
don't consciously set a goal to succeed
either. Instead you set these goals by
default, and once set, they become part
of who you are, and you perform to
their level. Beware of default goals!

> *Beware of where*
> *your mind*
> *wanders.*
> *Your words and*
> *actions follow.*

The Purpose of Goals

Create Cognitive Dissonance (Dissatisfaction)

As stated earlier, goals are designed to take you out of your comfort zone by creating dissatisfaction in your subconscious mind. When

you hold two conflicting thoughts, beliefs or opinions in your mind, it creates a state so uncomfortable that your subconscious mind seeks to reduce the conflict. It does so by altering one or both thoughts so that they fit together better. This condition is called cognitive dissonance.

Thus goals stimulate your creative juices into action to find a way to resolve this conflict. The more time you spend looking at your goals, reciting them and projecting yourself into the future through affirmations and visualization, the more powerfully and quickly you will assimilate the goal into your reality structure. It tells you "This is the way things are supposed to be."

The conflict comes between this picture of where you want to be and your current situation. You become dissatisfied being where you are, and your subconscious mind begins to search for creative ways to move you to this new vision that you are reinforcing regularly in your mind — this new, higher comfort zone.

Your subconscious mind alerts you so that you are more aware of things in your environment that will help resolve this conflict. Since your body can't tell the difference between a real experience and an imagined one, the more vividly and more often you imagine this new picture, the greater the dissatisfaction and the more powerful the search for a solution.

Remove Stress

This may sound contrary to the previous point, but it is actually not. Creating dissatisfaction in your subconscious motivates you to move out of your comfort zone and into a higher one. This is a positive stress as it prompts you to take action.

Stress is not beneficial if it creates anxiety that hinders your performance. But goals can also help remove anxiety. When your future is uncertain, there is a degree of stress — negative stress — that provides an underlying fear of the future. By setting goals and imagining yourself in the future, you are taking a certain degree of control of that future.

Provide Direction

There's a saying in education that "The winds don't favor the ship that has no port of destination." In other words, if you don't know where you're going, you're liable to end up somewhere else. You want to know where you're headed, and you need to keep the final destination in mind. You will not get to the major leagues by chance. Regardless of your talent, a career in the major leagues must be a driving force, and goals help to keep your passion level high and keep the energy and focus directed.

Properly set goals provide the framework for your future. They provide the parameters you can use for making decisions. When confronted with any situation, you can ask yourself, "Will this thought, behavior, action, etc., help me meet my goals or hinder them?" Whether it is on the field, off the field, in the locker room, selecting your breakfast at a restaurant, or deciding on that extra beer, all actions and behaviors can be measured against your goals and how they will affect the end result. This makes your choices simple: "Does it help me or not?"

Key Concepts to Successful Goal Setting

Stretch Goals, Aim High

Goals need to challenge and motivate you to new heights, to stretch your comfort zone. To aim high, it is important that you set your goal before you develop a strategy to accomplish it. Over the years I've noticed that players not only thrive, but are ultimately happier and more passionate about the game and their lives when they have a higher standard to strive toward. The more focused they become about their goals, the more energy they have.

> *...ᴛᴴᴱ greater danger for most of us is not that our aim is too high and we miss it, but that it is too low and we reach it.*
>
> MICHAEL ANGELO

If you are heading out on a hike, you probably won't end up on the mountain's summit unless that becomes your goal. Remember, the lower elevations are filled with day hikers, those who would love to scale the mountain but don't have the passion to do what's necessary. They are not willing to pay the price to reach the summit. You need to separate yourself from the day hikers and set your eyes on the summit. You need goals that are big enough to ignite your passion — big enough to get out of bed each day with excitement and anticipation. Too many players have a goal of getting to the big leagues. Not many have the goal of dominating at the big league level. Even fewer have the goal of being enshrined in the Hall of Fame. Aim high! Don't sell yourself short.

Be Specific

The more specific a goal, the more powerful it is. Too often players have goals that don't provide the fire they need to stay highly motivated for an entire season. If you want goals to be powerful, they need to be clear and focused. I cannot overstate the power of focus.

Remember being a child and using a magnifying glass on a sunny day to start a paper on fire? You used the glass to focus the suns rays onto the paper. Imagine your goal is what provides the light. The magnifying glass is your focus — what makes your goal powerful. To take the example even further, lasers take these light beams and focus them so minutely that the laser can cut through steel. Now that's focus, and focus equals power.

Write It Down

Most players I've met with over my 17 years in baseball state that they have goals. Most of the time these "goals" would be described more as dreams or wishes or good ideas. If they're not written down, these aims and ambitions are too vague for the mind to grasp in such a way that will provide the passion needed to accomplish them.

Besides providing passion, committing goals to paper takes them out of the mind and puts them in the physical realm where we live and operate in our day-to-day lives. Committing goals to paper also allows you to examine them to determine if they meet all the criteria of a good goal — measurable, specific, etc.

You gain a new perspective on your goals once you write them down. You can break them down into sub-goals, devise action plans, analyze them, update them and even reset them if needed, based on changing circumstances. And always remember that they are written on paper, not carved in granite. In baseball, circumstances — many beyond your control — may require you to adapt your goals or even alter them completely to meet changing circumstances, and that's just fine.

Once written down and reviewed regularly, your goals give your subconscious mind something to work with. When goals are on paper and broken into sub-goals, you can develop an action plan that will move you steadily toward your desired end.

Make Them Measurable

Goals need to be written in such a way that they are measurable so you can monitor your progress. If you find you are not moving toward your goal, you can adapt your behaviors. A goal such as "I want to be in the major leagues" is too vague to be measured. But a goal like "I will make my major league debut on September 1, 20XX" is easily both measureable and motivational. With this goal, each year you have a measuring stick to see if your movement is on schedule. Each day you can measure whether you made forward progress from the previous day. Another measurable goal might be "I will increase my quality at bats from 40 percent to 70 percent between now and the end of the year." Again you have something that's easy to evaluate. Are you a better player today than you were yesterday because of your actions? The answer to this question will tell you whether you're making progress.

Make Them Attainable

Aiming high is important, but goals also have to be realistic and achievable. You make lofty goals achievable and attainable by breaking them down into bite-sized pieces. You always want to keep your ultimate goal in mind, but you can't do your ultimate goal today. You can only do activities to accomplish goals today. Have short-term goals, and be sure to write out the activities you need to do to accomplish each goal.

Using Goals Properly

Goals that are properly thought out, written down, and measurable are a great start, but they won't help you if you don't use them properly. You must use them daily, so you need to make them part of your routine. You should read them a minimum of twice a day. Ideally, each morning and evening would work well in establishing a routine.

There are many ways to bring your goals to mind on a regular basis — write them into a journal or log book (more about this later), make them your computer screen saver, write them on a 3" x 5" card that you can carry with you, put them on your cell phone, put them on a sticky note in your car, put a colorful sticky dot on your watch, write them in soap on the mirror you use every morning, put an alarm on your watch at a set time each day, etc. Use your imagination to create ways to remind you to review your goals daily.

Another thing you can do to make these goals even more powerful is to read them out loud with passion and conviction. Do this when you're alone, so you can put emotion into it. The more emotion involved, the quicker the goal will be imbedded in your subconscious.

The purpose of this chapter was to lay the framework to help you develop a mental picture of your future performance. The following chapters will provide suggestions and tools to imprint your goals on your subconscious through the affirmation and visualization process.

Your Turn

Taking the time to properly consider and write out your goals will prepare you for the upcoming chapters.

List several Ultimate goals:

Goal 1:_____

_____

Goal 2: _____

_____

Goal 3: _____

_____

List several Outcome goals:

Goal 1:_____

_____

Goal 2: _____

_____

Goal 3: _____

_____

List several Process goals:

Goal 1:_____

_____

Goal 2: _____

_____

Goal 3: _____

_____

Now stop to consider what might be some default goals you have set without meaning to, ones that could be hindering your performance?

Negative Goal 1:_____

_____

Negative Goal 2: _____

_____

Negative Goal 3: _____

_____

In Sum...

- As humans we have the ability to project into the future. Goals are a powerful way to use this ability to identify and influence future behaviors and future performances.

- There are three types of goals that are consciously set and can influence future performances in a positive way: ultimate goals, outcome goals and process goals.

- The fourth type of goals, default goals, are set subconsciously and are generally negative and counter productive. They work against your consciously set goals and hinder performance.

- Properly written goals should provide direction and energize and inspire you to action.

PART 3

The Four Basic
Mental Skills

Baseball's 6th Tool — the mental game — can be described as a tool kit made up of a variety of equipment to help you achieve your goals. Where Part 2 helped identify changes you should make to move toward a brighter future, Part 3 provides the skills necessary to make these changes: (1) relaxation, (2) affirmations, (3) mental recall and (4) mental rehearsal.

In Chapter 7 you will be introduced to relaxation techniques and how relaxation places you into the alpha state — the perfect mental state to make the changes you want to accomplish. Then in Chapters 8, 9 and 10, you will learn how to activate your entire brain to bring change quickly and permanently. These three chapters apply the right brain/left brain theory developed by Nobel Prize-winner Roger W. Sperry. He discovered that your brain is divided into two parts. Each side of the brain has a dominant and different way of thinking than the other side. The right brain is more visual, intuitive and creative, and the left-brain is more logical, analytical, sequential and language focused.

Research has shown that although each hemisphere has its dominant functions, we learn and function most effectively when both halves work in harmony. Think of your brain operating much like your hands. If you are right handed, you automatically use the right hand for many tasks because it is the dominant of the two. The same applies for left-handed people. That doesn't mean the non-dominant hand is useless. If you used only your dominant hand, many tasks would be more difficult and often impossible. Using both hands increases your efficiency and makes most tasks easier. The brain operates similarly so it only makes sense to activate both hemispheres to make change easier and quicker.

Chapter 8 will focus on how you activate the left hemisphere of your brain, the logical portion, through the use of affirmations. The term "affirmations" for our purposes will mean controlled "self-talk" that focuses on characteristics and behaviors you need to exhibit to meet your goals.

Chapters 9 and 10 will focus on how to bring in the right hemisphere, the creative portion, through the use of visualization. Chapter 9, the chapter on mental recall, will discuss how you build on past successes, while Chapter 10, mental rehearsal, emphasizes how to project into the future and imagine your success.

Players often use mental recall or mental rehearsal while neglecting or offsetting any benefit through negative self-talk or vice versa. That means they are using only a portion of the resources at their disposal, and the results are usually less than satisfactory.

It's important to incorporate both the affirmation process (logical brain) and the visualization process (creative brain) because each one activates a different portion of your brain. Using this model activates the *entire* brain so that both hemispheres work together toward your new goals.

CHAPTER 7

Relaxation:
The Power of Letting Go

*"Tension is who you think you should be.
Relaxation is who you are."*

Chinese Proverb

The first of the skills you must master to lay the foundation for your mental training program is the ability to relax. Besides the obvious benefit of being able to control stress levels and emotional spikes during competition while remaining mentally alert, regular relaxation provides many additional benefits that can improve performance. If you did nothing else but master this particular skill, you would improve your game — and your life — dramatically. Although our focus will be on using relaxation as the first of the four foundations skills for mental training, I'll also present the other benefits you can derive from regular relaxation.

From the mental training standpoint, relaxation places you in a state where your subconscious is most receptive to suggestion, thus speeding up the process of setting your reticular activating system (RAS) on a new course. Keep in mind that the relaxed state prepares the mind for mental imagery.

Opening the Subconscious Mind for Change

You'll recall from previous chapters that your self-image, which drives all behaviors, was established through accepting suggestions that you gave it, or that others suggested and you that you then took as fact. You also saw that applying the same process of repeating suggestions and acceptance of new images and behaviors is how you alter the self-image. Since one of the goals of The 6th Tool is to make the desired change rapidly, you want to use everything at your disposal to speed up the process. Therefore, you want the subconscious mind in the most receptive state, a relaxed condition called the alpha state.

It is the alpha state that opens the door to your subconscious mind, where you are aware yet not actively thinking. You enter this state naturally when you are sleepy or drowsy and you can enter it purposely through relaxation, meditation or hypnosis. Research has shown that this is the ideal state for reprogramming your subconscious mind with both affirmations and visual imagery to improve performance and change behaviors.

In this relaxed state, the alpha state, your rational mind, which resists change, is quieted. It is the rational mind that tells you, "I can't because . . .!" It's that part of your mind that argues for your limitations. It simply does not want change. The role of the rational mind is to keep you just the way you are, in your comfort zone. So when coaches ask you to try altering your swing or changing your position on the rubber, your rational mind immediately focuses on how uncomfortable it is, how it doesn't "feel right." This is its attempt to keep you in your comfort zone. This resistance to change occurs at the beta level. See Figure 7-1 for an explanation of the various states of consciousness.

When you enter the alpha state, either through relaxation techniques or naturally, you more readily accept the input you feed the mind through affirmations and imagery. You accept this input with complete conviction because in the alpha state — where your body can't tell the difference between a real experience and an imagined one — you accept the new images as the real you, unencumbered by the rational mind.

To illustrate how your subconscious mind accepts information without assessing it, I will share an experience I had during my college

FIGURE 7-1

States of Consciousness

Brain Frequency in Cycles per Second (CPS)

Your brain operates electrically, like a computer, in wavelengths and frequencies commonly measured in cycles per second (CPS). Fast electrical vibrations occur above 20 CPS, and below 10 you are in a very relaxed state conducive to imagery.

Beta 14–40 CPS	Conscious state. Awake and alert. Associated with left-brain thinking (logical). Low levels of beta (under 17 CPS) are where you play in a relaxed but focused state. You are in the present moment. In mid levels, where you spend much of your day, you are actively aware, thinking, etc. When in upper levels (25 CPS and above) you get into deep thinking. These upper levels are where excessive inner chatter and high stress occur. You fluctuate within the beta range during most of the day based on alertness. Above 20 CPS you are very alert, while in the lower level of range you are less alert.
Alpha 7–14 CPS	Relaxed state. Drowsy at the 14 CPS level and getting more relaxed as CPS lowers. Associated with right-brain thinking (visualizing). Receptive state for imagery/visualization.
Theta 4–7 CPS	Deeply relaxed state and the light sleep state. REM sleep occurs in this state. Creative visualizing also occurs during this state as the mind wanders.
Delta 0.5–3.5	Non-dreaming deep sleep. Mind is at complete rest. Rejuvenation, recovery and healing occur at this level. Unconscious state.

years. Late one night in the dorm while most everyone else was asleep, several students came back from downtown, where adult beverages were the norm. They walked down the hall shouting, "FIRE! FIRE! GET OUT OF THE BUILDING!" Doors flew open, and students in various states of undress ran toward the exit. It took most of them several seconds before they were alert and conscious enough to assess the situation realistically. There was no smoke, no alarm, and several of their friends and colleagues were rolling on the floor in laughter. This happened because, during sleep, their conscious minds were shut down and they accepted the suggestion without consciously checking for an alarm or smoke.

Your level of consciousness affects how readily you accept suggestions. When you systematically imprint suggestions on your subconscious while in the alpha state, your mind accepts that information without questioning its validity. Since you often enter this state naturally when tired, one suggestion is to do your affirmations and imagery immediately before getting out of bed in the morning or in the evening at bedtime when you are most likely to be in this state without extra effort. Intentional relaxation, meditation and self-hypnosis are other ways to achieve the alpha state. As a certified sports hypnotist, I often use hypnosis when working with players. However, in this chapter, the focus will be on basic relaxation to prep you for the next step.

Another point to keep in mind is that after a game, when lying in bed before you fall asleep, you are in this receptive state. Often this is the time that players recall previous events from the game, often many being negative — times where they failed. These negative thoughts taking place in the alpha state are more powerful than at any other time, and they will affect the consistency of your performance in the future, but not in the way you'd like. Take control of your thoughts at all times, especially when you are in this receptive state and be sure to keep them focused positively on your goals.

Benefits of Relaxation

As an added incentive to encourage regular relaxation, I'd like to list and briefly discuss other benefits you will gain when you just learn to relax.

Every ballplayer can benefit from regular relaxation both on and off the field. Research has shown that benefits occur when you practice regular relaxation, which in research studies means daily practice.

Ability to Concentrate

Placing yourself in a relaxed state helps develop your ability to concentrate because you actually practice concentration each time you relax. Relaxation requires you to focus your attention and tune out distractions. You train your body to concentrate and to increase focus at your conscious command.

You tend to lose focus when you get fatigued. As you become more proficient at relaxing and you get more deeply relaxed, it is easy to drift off into a sleep that mimics a mentally exhaustive state. When using relaxation for imagery, you don't want to drift off, so you have to concentrate more to prevent yourself from falling asleep, thus you practice focusing even while in a state of fatigue.

Many techniques require intense focus within your body to feel sensations and feelings that are often difficult to sense or isolate. Hence, you are perfecting your focus and tuning out distractions along with the ability to relax. Standard autogenic training (SAT) is one of the best techniques that provide this dual benefit, improved focus while practicing relaxation. Detailed instructions on how to implement SAT are provided in Appendix B.

Control Emotional Spikes

Research also illustrates that people who relax on a daily basis have greater psychological and physiological control of their bodies' arousal levels than do those who do not relax daily. For many play-

> *A ballplayer who loses his head and can't keep his cool is worse than no player at all.*
>
> LOU GEHRIG

ers, lack of emotional control takes them out of their game. It may simply be a bad bounce, poor fielding behind them, or a perceived poor call by an umpire that sets off an emotional spike where the player gets frustrated and/or angry.

Regular relaxation helps eliminate or at least lessen emotional spikes. What's more, if such a spike does occur, people who relax regularly are able to get back in balance within seconds with instant relaxation techniques. You can use these techniques during a game without anyone knowing. They can help you refocus and quickly get back to your perfect physical and psychological level of control if you've strayed from that level.

Reduce Physical Recovery Time

Following physical exercise, muscles need time to recover and to filter out the waste products. The more exhaustive the exercise, the more time needed to remove these metabolic waste products. In the relaxed state, blood vessels in the arms, hands, legs and feet dilate, increasing the circulation to these areas and speeding up the removal of these waste products. This in turn reduces recovery time from exercise and speeds up healing following an injury.

Improving Sleep

Relaxation can also be used to improve sleep. People who relax effectively sleep more quickly as well as more soundly. When relaxing you increase your focus on specific body parts — feelings, sensations and the like — and allow your mind to shut down and enter the sleep state. Additionally, when you fall asleep in a relaxed state, you awake more refreshed because your body has been in a relaxed state throughout the night.

Reduces Illnesses

Another benefit of relaxation is that it strengthens your immune system. For years it has been known that stress weakens the immune system and makes you more susceptible to colds, the flu or flare-ups of any weak system you have in your body such as ulcers, asthma, etc. Regular relaxation counteracts this weakening and actually places your body in a state that is more conductive to good health.

Improves Relationships and Social Satisfaction

People who relax get along better with others, both in the home setting as well as in the work setting, than they did prior to beginning a relaxation program. Relaxation reduces stress, which brings about more patience, better health, and better sleep as indicated above. All of these allow you to be more effective in social settings. Stressed people tend to be the ones to have the emotional spikes, blow up, make inappropriate comments, etc.

Develops Better Body Awareness

In the relaxed state you learn to tune into your body and what's occurring within. As an athlete you get a better reading on your body, which can benefit you in several ways. First, when you work out you can push yourself to the limit by listening to your body. On the converse side, greater body awareness allows you to monitor aches and pains with a greater understanding of their seriousness. This allows you to back off so you don't overdo things and will help you to better discern any serious problems more quickly.

Relaxation Techniques

There are hundreds if not thousands of ways to achieve relaxation. In this chapter I'll present several relaxation techniques, all of which incorporate connecting the breathing rhythm with relaxation.

As an athlete, it is important to connect relaxation to the breathing cycle for several reasons. First, the exhalation phase of your breathing cycle is your body's built-in relaxation phase. If you focus on your exhalations for three or four breaths, you'll notice a feeling of your body sinking down, slowing down and/or becoming heavy. All are related to relaxation.

Second, during games, you want to be in the present so that you are highly focused. Being in the present moment shuts down your thinking and clears your mind. Since your breathing is always in the present, focusing on your breathing brings you to the present and — with practice — clears your mind.

Third, you eventually want to be able to relax in one or two breaths so that you can control your stress level during a game and stay at the level where you perform at your best. With practice, the quickest way to do this is to take a breath, exhale, relax and move to the desired level. And you can do so without anyone knowing you were stressed or a little out of sorts in the first place.

Guidelines for Using Your Breathing to Relax

1. Breathe normally. Passively observe what your body does as you inhale and exhale. Allow your body to breathe by itself as if you were a bystander.

2. Focus only on your exhalations. The relaxation phase of your breathing is the exhalation phase. Try it now. Take a deep breath, hold it for a second, and notice the letting go of body tension as you exhale.

3. Feel and experience key sensations of relaxation as you exhale, AND ONLY AS YOU EXHALE. Feel the sensations

of sinking down, slowing down, heaviness, warmth, letting go, contentment and comfort.

Try It!

Linking Technique — Anchoring Relaxation to Your Breathing

Read through the entire exercise before you do it.

1. Sit in a comfortable position.

2. Passively observe your breathing for approximately 1 minute.

3. After observing your exhalations only,

    a. Take 3-4 breaths to feel (or notice) your body sinking down with each exhalation, *only* during the exhalation.

    b. Take 3-4 breaths to notice your body slowing down as you exhale.

    c. Take 3-4 breaths to notice heaviness in your body as you exhale.

4. Take a deep breath, flex and stretch, and open your eyes.

Through this exercise, you have linked the relaxation phase of your breathing cycle, the exhalation phase, with certain feelings of relaxation — the sinking down, slowing down and heaviness. Combining the two provides a compounding effect that carries you quickly to a calm state. With practice you should be able to feel each of these sensations within one breath. Once you've learned to connect your exhalations to these feelings within one breath, you're ready to move on to the exhalation exercise.

The Exhalation Exercise

The exhalation exercise will continue strengthening the connection between your breathing and relaxation. It will take you to a deeper state of relaxation using the same guidelines as above. This time, you'll also experience the sensations of letting go and warmth, and you will spend more time on each feeling, which will take you to a deeper state.

You can go to the website **baseballs6thtool.com** to download a free audio copy of the exhalation exercise to play on your iPod or computer. This is also the relaxation exercise used as Step 1 of the Mindset for Winning (MFW) audio programs. The MFW programs are available on the website for both position players and for pitchers.

Try it!

Exhalation Exercise

Read through the entire exercise below before you do it. Use the same guidelines regarding breathing as listed earlier.

1. Get into a comfortable position, either sitting or lying down.

2. Close your eyes and passively observe your breath, noticing the air as it enters and leaves your nose/mouth. Notice the coolness of the air as it enters and the warmth as you exhale. Do this for approximately one minute.

3. Take 4-6 breaths to feel your body **sinking down** as you exhale.

4. For 4-6 breaths, feel your body **slowing down** as you exhale. You may notice your heart rate or breathing slow down, or just a sense of slowing down throughout.

5. For 4-6 breaths, focus on the feeling of **heaviness** as you exhale. You may notice it in your arms, possibly your legs, or in the trunk of your body. Simply notice it and focus on it each time you exhale.

6. For 4-6 breaths, notice and feel **warmth** somewhere in your body. When you notice it, focus on it during each exhalation.

Great job! You now know how to relax using your breathing as an anchor!

Sequential Relaxation

There are two approaches to relaxation. Mind-body relaxation is one approach. The second is the opposite — body-mind relaxation. Both have the same result — relaxation! The exhalation exercise you just did is a mind-body technique and works most of the time for most people. However, if you have a mind that races and you can't turn it off, a body-mind technique works best.

Sequential relaxation is a body-mind technique that is great for when you can't turn off your thought process. It's also a great technique to use to go to sleep when your mind is racing.

During the sequential technique, you use the exhalation phase of the breathing and couple it with specific body parts to relax. You focus on a body part for several exhalations relaxing those muscles, then, you move in sequence through the body doing the same with each muscle group.

Try it!
Sequential Relaxation

Read through the entire exercise below before you do it. Use the same guidelines regarding breathing as presented earlier.

1. Get into a comfortable position, either sitting or lying down.

2. Close your eyes and passively observe your breathing, noticing the air as it enters and leaves your nose/mouth.

3. Notice the coolness of the air as it enters your nose/mouth

and the warmth of the air as you exhale. Do this for 4-5 breaths.

4. Focus on a specific body part. For the sake of simplicity I recommend the following sequence:

    a. right foot, then left foot

    b. right lower leg (calf region), then left lower leg

    c. right upper leg (thigh), then left upper leg

    d. hips/buttocks

    e. trunk (including shoulders)

    f. right arm, then left arm

    g. right hand, then left hand

5. Focusing on one body part at a time, notice a sinking down and heavy feeling for 3-4 breaths each. Then move on. Move quickly, but breath normally. Do not rush, but move on after every 3-4 breaths regardless of whether you feel the sensation. Keep your mind busy looking for those feelings.

6. Move through your body in the sequence suggested or until you feel relaxed.

7. When you are finished, come out of the relaxed state like you are waking up in the morning. Take a deep breath and simultaneously flex, then stretch and open your eyes.

Instant Relaxation

Instant relaxation (IR) refers to a variety of techniques that can help you immediately control arousal level and emotional spikes that occur during a game. They are short, generally 5 to 20 seconds long and, although they do not place you in a deeply relaxed state, they offer many advantages and complement your mental skills. I've taught many IR techniques to players but will only present a few to illustrate these types of technique and how they can be used.

The main benefit is that these skills can actually be used during a game without others knowing you're relaxing. They are quick and easy to do and can be used to lower your stress level, get back on track after an emotional spike (regain composure), and get you to that perfect tension level you need to perform at your best.

One player I worked with used IR between every pitch as he looked at the 3rd base coach to get the signs. Another used them while in the on-deck circle to get to the perfect tension level where he played at his best. Some pitchers use them between pitches after perfecting them to 1 breath in length, and the techniques help them focus better.

Although some techniques suggest a deep breath, during a game you'd want to perfect the technique you use so that you breathe normally and rather than taking a deep breath if others are observing you. Taking several deep breaths sends a non-verbal message that you are stressed. You need to relax on a regular basis away from the park in a non-stressful environment to perfect these skills so they work in the stressful environment without a deep breath.

All IR techniques require that you've learned to connect your breathing cycle — the exhalation phase with feelings of relaxation. This is the connection that is established with regular practice of the relaxation techniques listed earlier in this chapter.

Try it!
The R and R Technique (Relax and Respond)

The R and R is a two–breath tension control technique that can be done in 5 to 10 seconds. The first exhalation is the relaxation portion while the second is the responding phase.

1. The relaxation breath: Focusing on your first breath, inhale, then slowly exhale and allow your body to relax and sink down as you feel the gentle pull of gravity. Just let go of all tension on this exhalation.

2. The response breath: Take a second breath and as you exhale, respond (return to your activity — i.e., focus on the glove, the pitcher, the situation, an affirmation, etc.)

The Deep Breath Technique

This is a one-breath technique that would be used most effectively in the on-deck circle, the dugout, or in the field when you are not the focal point. It can be repeated several times to get you to the desired level of relaxation, but use a deep breath only on the first breath. If repeated, each successive breath should be a normal breath and not a deep breath.

1. Take in a deep breath, hold it for several seconds, and as you exhale feel your body sinking down, letting go and relaxing.

2. Repeat as necessary to get to the proper tension level.

The Stretch Technique

This IR technique uses stretching to create muscle tension and then incorporates the exhalation phase to relax your body.

1. Take a deep breath and stretch, creating tension in the hands, arms and chest.

2. As you exhale, release the tension.

3. Breath normally on the next inhalation.

4. As you exhale, mentally scan your body for any remaining tension and let it go on this exhalation.

In sum...

- Relaxation is the first of the four foundation steps of a mental skills program.

- Deep relaxation techniques, such as the exhalation exercise and sequential relaxation, place you in the alpha state — the most effective state in which to change beliefs and behaviors. These techniques also help establish the connection between the exhalation phase of your breathing and the feelings associated with relaxation.

- Besides preparing you for mental skills, there are eight additional benefits an athlete can receive from regular relaxation: improved ability to concentrate, controlling emotional spikes, reducing recovery time, improving sleep, reduced minor illnesses, improved relationships and social satisfaction, and improved body awareness.

- Instant relaxation techniques are techniques that take seconds to do and can be done anywhere in any environment, including during a game, without others realizing you are relaxing. They help you reduce your tension and arousal level during times when you can't do deep relaxation.

CHAPTER 8

Activating Your Left Brain: The Affirmation Process

"Whatever is true, whatever is honorable,
whatever is just, whatever is pure, whatever is lovely,
whatever is gracious, if there is any excellence,
if there is anything worthy of praise,
think about those things."

Philippians 4:8

I pose the following question to players when I meet with them for the first time: "If your best friend talked to you the way you talk to yourself, would that person be still be your best friend?" More often than not it brings a revealing smile to their face that tells me what I need to know. Most players do not realize or even think about their inner chatter — their self-talk — and how powerful these thoughts and words can be. Your self-talk, how you think, and how you talk to yourself has a tremendous effect on both your confidence and your performance. Zig Zigler, an internationally known motivational speaker and author, emphasized this power when he stated, "You are what you are because of what goes into your mind."

Words have a powerful effect, and no words are more powerful than those you speak to yourself. Self-talk, self-thought, inner chatter or whatever you call it takes place constantly throughout the day. It's estimated that thousands of conversations take place in your head on a daily basis. Behavioral research has found that for the average person, 77 percent of these thoughts are negative.

These conversations take on many forms — thoughts or ideas popping in, conversations taking place, asking a question, answering the question or making statements. They take place everywhere — in the car, in bed, during meetings and, yes, on the mound, in the on-deck circle, in the batters' box, on the bench and in the field. Absolutely no place is off limits to these inner conversations.

Kirk Gibson, current manager of the Arizona Diamondbacks, in his book titled *"Bottom of the Ninth,"* discusses how he went from a miserable season in 1983 to having a complete turnaround in 1984 — a change that fueled his future. He used negative self-talk and explained how he changed it.

"When coming to bat in the bottom of the ninth, with the game on the line and a tough pitcher on the mound, I would say to myself, "My God, this guy is nasty. I don't want to make the last out of the game. I don't want to strike out."

"It was like filing a flight plan for disaster. If success occurred in such a situation it was purely by accident."

After learning how to incorporate affirmations and visualizations, he went on to describe his new self-talk.

"...Now, if I struck out in a key situation, I would say to myself, 'That's not like me,' and I would begin to imprint a positive image in my mind, rubbing out the old one.... 'I love pressure situations. I perform even better under these circumstances." There's the affirmation. Now, I follow up with the visualization. I see myself in a packed stadium with the game on the line, hitting a home run off Goose Gossage to win the game. I can visualize such a moment very clearly."

Self-talk is important. If you recall from Chapter 2, self-talk is at the top of the self-image cycle. This is where you can most effectively begin the intervention process to influence inner beliefs. It is a great tool for improving behaviors, strengthening confidence, boosting self-image and stretching your comfort zone to a new high.

The Major Problem with Self-Talk:
The Avoidance Syndrome

The most common mistake players make in their self-talk is to focus on behaviors they want to avoid. Examples of this could include thoughts such as "Don't strike out here," "Don't boot this ball," "Don't hang this curveball," "I can't walk this guy," or "I hope they don't hit it to me." Since all inner conversations paint a picture for your body to follow, you are more likely to display the negative behavior suggested in your self-talk than the behavior that you consciously want to enact. The avoidance syndrome is focusing on the hole, not the donut!

Here's an example of two different ways of saying the same thing — one paints a positive picture while the other focuses on avoidance by painting a negative picture. If I state, "Don't spill the milk!" what comes to mind? Spilt milk! The same thing said in a positive way — "Be careful with the milk!" — creates an image of someone walking carefully as they carry the milk. The way you phrase things, even when you talk to yourself, completely changes the image that comes to mind.

Your mind paints pictures, but it has difficulty creating appropriate pictures for certain words — "don't," "no," "can't," "not," and "shouldn't" may conjure negative images. They aren't affirmative words, so keep them out of your affirmations.

Rephrase your negative self-talk by changing your inner thoughts. For example, rather than stating, "Don't strike out here," change it to "Drive the ball into the gap." Instead of "Don't walk this batter," say "Attack the K zone down and in." You get the idea.

When your thoughts focus on what you want to avoid, two things happen. First, you increase the chances of doing exactly what you don't want to do because you've created the wrong image in your mind. Second, by focusing on the negative, you have created a thought pattern that erodes your confidence and creates more stress, anxiety and nervousness.

Players who excel when the pressure is on are those who channel the adrenalin and the accompanying stress into increased focus and concentration. At the same time, they remain relatively relaxed physically. They have learned to control their inner chatter and even to turn it off when they need to do so.

Writing Affirmations

Affirmations can be written several ways. They can be short phrases or sentences that focus on a specific behavior or trait. Or they can be lengthier, from a sentence to a paragraph, and encompass several behaviors. However you choose to write your affirmations, the following guidelines will help you develop this important performance skill. In Chapter 11, I'll show you several ways to incorporate these affirmations into a mental practice routine.

Guidelines for Writing Affirmations

1. **Affirmations need to be based on your goals and desired behaviors.**

   Affirmations should be based on your goals and the desired behaviors you must accomplish to achieve your goals. Write at least one affirmation for each goal, behavior or thought pattern you want to change.

2. **Affirmations need to be positive.**

   Champions focus on what they want to happen, not on what they want to avoid. With this in mind, write your affirmation using positive wording.

   For example, the statement, "I am not nervous or anxious when on the mound," focuses on the behavior you want to avoid, but if you just rephrase it — "I am confident and relaxed when on the mound" — you focus on the behavior you want to achieve. Let's look at another example, first an avoidance statement, "I don't swing at pitchers out of the strike zone," and then a true, positive affirmation, "I am patient and selective at the plate."

3. **Use the present tense with "I am" statements.**

    Use language in your affirmations that projects the image and behaviors you want to develop, stated as if you already possess them. Statements such as "I am..." or "I have..." tell the subconscious mind that you already possess these qualities — a much more powerful thought than suggesting you may achieve these qualities in the future.

4. **Use positive adjectives that generate emotions.**

    When you write affirmations, choose action words that have meaning for you and evoke an emotional response, words such as powerful, strong, relentless, attack and awesome. These are more likely to generate an emotional response than words that are more docile.

    A statement such as "I feel powerful and strong" is more effective than "I feel good," just like "My arm feels awesome" is more encouraging than "My arm feels fine." Figure 8-1 list examples of words that will help you write more powerful affirmations — if, that is, they create a response for you. Everyone is different. Personalize your affirmations.

FIGURE 8-1
Powerful Affirmation Words

Amazing	Drive	Persistent
Aggressive	Enthusiastic	Powerful
Attack	Excited	Relentless
Awesome	Explode	Sensational
Battle	Fabulous	Spectacular
Commanding	Gutsy	Strong
Confident	Overpowering	Stupendous
Dominate	Passionate	Successful

---

5. **Use cause and effect wording.**

A powerful way to tie thoughts together is to use a cause/effect statement. For example, "Because I work hard and stay positive [cause], I am confident at the plate [effect]." Or, "When the coach signals a pick [cause], it causes me to relax, focus and make a strong, accurate throw to first [effect]."

6. **Make your affirmations personal.**

You need to create your own affirmations. They must be based on your goals and the behaviors and traits that will help *you* achieve *your* goals. The words used in the affirmation must have personal meaning and project a positive image or picture in your mind. Make them yours!

7. **Suggest something better**

You don't want affirmations to limit your potential so I suggest you add the phrase "or better" to affirmations that are result oriented — and do the same with your result goals. So a goal of having a .310 batting average or an affirmation such as "I have a .310 batting average" could limit the upside unless you add "or better" to the end.

Sample Affirmations

The following affirmations illustrate how they can be written for specific behaviors or characteristics. All of the affirmations presented in this chapter are samples only, examples of how to write affirmations that will have the most power to affect your game for the better. They merely serve as guidelines to help you build your own affirmations based on (1) your needs and (2) your own terminology.

Sample Affirmations for Players

For Confidence

• "I am confident and positive in everything I do. On game days

I expect great results because I am healthy. I have prepared properly, and I have a solid game plan."

- "I choose to do everything I can to maximize my talent. Therefore, to develop my talents, I *always* remains confident, I always control my attitude, and I always give 100 percent effort. As a professional, I develop both my mental game and my physical game, and I come to the park each day with a mental game plan."

- "I am confident. My arm feels awesome, and I feel great. When I take the mound, I am completely relaxed, and I walk and feel tall. When I pitch, I am relaxed, accurate, consistent, and I attack the strike zone. On each pitch, I automatically keep my weight back and get my leg out first."

Notice how this affirmation brings in a variety of behaviors. First is health followed by the body language this player exhibits when playing at his best, then how he feels when he's at the top of his game, and finally the mechanics he wants to make automatic.

For Health and Healing

- "My body is a powerful healing machine."

- "I know that being positive strengthens my immune system and creates better health, vitality and energy. Therefore, I choose to be positive in my self-talk and in my conversations with others. I expect health and healing."

- "I choose to activate my subconscious mind with positive affirmations, positive self-talk and visualization. I feel God's healing power within my body, and I fully expect my body to respond to my visualizations of health and wellness."

Note: Here the affirmation combines healthful thoughts as well as stating a behavior — visualization.

Samples for Position Players

For Accuracy in Throwing

- "I field the ball, focus on my target, and throw instinctively, firmly and accurately to that target."

- "My throw follows my sight. I focus on the target and trust my body to deliver the throw accurately to the exact spot I see."

For Success at the Plate

- "I am a great hitter, and I am always confident at the plate, expecting wonderful results. I feel that short, compact, quick and powerful swing, and I feel the ball explode off of my bat."

- "My body, my hands and my bat stay behind the ball, and I feel the power generated by staying back. I see the backspin carry the ball into the gap."

Note: Each player has different approaches, feelings and goals for when he plays at his best. The affirmation here reflects this player's approach when he is playing best.

Samples for Pitchers

For Pitching Confidence

- "I have complete confidence in all of my pitches. When on the mound, I feel comfortable and I pitch aggressively to contact, knowing that I am at my best when I attack the strike zone."

- "When on the mound I feel strong, confident and I focus on the positive at all times. I stand tall, walk tall and pitch with the body language of a warrior, knowing that 'I'm the Man.'"

Note: This player performed at his best and was most confident when he projected this body language.

For Throwing Strikes

- "I have complete confidence in and control of all of my pitches. I am accurate, and I consistently throw first-pitch strikes."

- "I am a great control pitcher because I throw first-pitch strikes, and I attack the strike zone."

For Developing a New Pitch

- "Because I know that growth only occurs with change, I choose to develop my change-up. I know this pitch will add to my success so I practice it, I visualize it, and I choose to throw it in game situations. I love the challenge of developing this pitch because it takes my game to a whole new level."

Samples for Catchers

For Blocking

- "I am confident behind the plate. I instinctively move to block the ball and, like a magnet, I block it and it stays within my grasp."

- "I instinctively block strike 3, and I move quickly and powerfully to the ball, pick it, and rifle an accurate throw to first base."

Note: This example was for a catcher who had trouble throwing to first after a strike out.

For Throwing

- "I throw the ball back to the pitcher accurately, powerfully, firmly, with authority and without thought."

General Affirmations

Affirmations can be used for everything — from general to specific. Listed here are several of my favorites. The first one is one of the earliest and probably the most famous affirmation, which was written by Emile Coule, a French psychologist. He was the first to suggest that people use affirmations to set their subconscious mind for success, health and happiness. It's general and encompasses everything in life.

- "Every day, in every way, I am getting better and better."

Here is another general affirmation, which was shared with me by a former Notre Dame football player. It is one of my favorites. It was developed and used by Lou Holtz, former Notre Dame coach, when they won the 1987 NCAA Football Championship.

- "The momentum is always flowing my way."

That's a great thought to have in your mind even when things aren't flowing your way — *yet!* It tells your subconscious to search for something little to turn the tide in your direction.

Spiritual Affirmations

Spiritual affirmations can be extremely powerful if you are a spiritual person because they incorporate your belief system. Historically, affirmations originated in the Bible, and the Bible emphasized the importance of your mind. The book of Proverbs is described as a book of affirmations and emphasizes that thoughts have creative ability. "For as he thinks in his heart, so is he." So if you want to lead a successful, joyous, happy, fulfilling life you need to control your thoughts. Not just in Proverbs, but throughout the Bible, statements and phrases appear that can be used as powerful affirmations.

I've found that when spiritual affirmations are incorporated by players who are strong spiritually, they tend to increase confidence and speed up the change process.

Biblical Affirmations

- "I can do all things through Christ who gives me strength." Phil 4:13

- "If Christ be for me, who can be against me." Romans 8:31

Joseph Murphy is the author of *The Power of Your Subconscious Mind* as well as the book *Think Yourself Rich*. The latter book focuses on affirmations from the spiritual standpoint used to develop a rich life, not necessarily monetary riches. The affirmation below is adapted from this book and illustrates how it can be used for baseball.

- "My business is God's business, and God's business always prospers. I am prospering in all areas of my life. Knowing that God is my partner, I am always confident, strive to give my best to display my God-given talent, and I always focus on the positive. Each night I review the wonderful blessings the Lord has given me throughout the day."

Each day you have thousands of thoughts and you have the ability to choose the right thoughts that will further your goals if you decide to do so. Remember, right thinking doesn't just happen. You are bombarded daily with lots of garbage that influences your thinking — through the media, TV, the music you listen to, negative people, etc. It becomes imperative to monitor your thoughts because they become habitual if similar thoughts are repeated.

This simple concept — controlling and directing your self-talk to paint a picture of what you want to happen and where you want to go — is key to keeping your confidence at a high level and your performance consistent. Your thoughts, words and actions are interconnected. Thoughts lead to words; words lead to actions and actions lead to results.

Mahatma Gandhi emphasized the importance of controlling

Thoughts → Words → Actions → Results

---

self-talk when he stated:

Keep my words positive, because my words become behaviors.

Keep my behaviors positive, because my behaviors become habits.

Keep my habits positive, because my habits become my values.

Keep my values positive, because they become my destiny.

It all begins with your thoughts and self-talk. They are one thing you have 100 percent control of — take that control!

Your Turn

Take one of your goals or a behavior you want to change (one you identified during the evaluation chapter), and then write an affirmation or two for that behavior or goal.

Behavior or Goal

Affirmation 1 _____

_____

_____

_____

Affirmation 2 _____

_____

_____

_____

Affirmation 3 _____

_____

_____

_____

How to Use Affirmations Effectively

Although it's important to write effective affirmations, you need to use them properly to see the greatest results. Following these guidelines will provide the most rapid results.

1. Read your affirmations a minimum of three times daily when you initially begin with a new one. After a week or two, cut back to twice a day. The key is consistency. I recommend that you read them in the morning immediately after you wake up and in the evening before you go to sleep as two of the sessions. Both times are ideal since you are most likely to be in the alpha state when relaxed. You should also use them before going to the park or at some other time that you can build into your day-to-day schedule.

2. After reading an affirmation, close your eyes and reflect on it for 30-40 seconds. Reflection may include just thinking about being that person or actually visualizing being that person. Or perhaps you might think about things you could do that day to become that person. If you are using multiple affirmations, after you are done with the first one, open your eyes, read the next one, reflect on it, and so on with each successive affirmation.

3. Keep the time short. You should do each affirmation includ-
    ing the refection 30 seconds to 1 minute.

4. *Don't force the issue!* Just read the affirmations and reflect on
    them three times daily and then *forget it!* Your subconscious
    mind is working 24/7. Let your subconscious do the rest. It
    will identify and alert you to opportunities to be that person.

5. Make the right choice! The affirmation process works when
    your subconscious alerts your conscious mind to the behav-
    iors and thought patterns you desire. Initially, you have to
    make a conscious choice to change. Continue this process
    until the changes become habitual.

In Sum...

- Inner chatter and self-talk are conversations you have in your
  head thousands of times a day. For the average person, 77 percent of these thoughts are negative, counterproductive and
  work against your goals.

- Habitual negative thoughts are a result of focusing on what
  you want to avoid, rather than on what you want to have happen.

- Simply rephrasing these inner thoughts and conversations
  through the affirmation process can produce an immediate
  and powerful positive effect on your behaviors and performance.

- For affirmations to be effective, they must be written correctly
  and used regularly to reset the RAS toward this new pattern.
  At the same time, don't force them — allow the change to
  come from within.

CHAPTER 9

Mental Recall:
Activating Your Right Brain

"Success breeds success."

Mia Hamm

You've learned to use the affirmation process to activate the left-brain, and now the visualization process will help you activate the right brain, completing the quest of summoning your entire brain to work toward your goals. I'll introduce you to two ways of visualization. In this chapter, we'll focus on the first type, mental recall, and in the next chapter, I'll explain the second type, mental rehearsal. Both are categorized under visualization, so I'll begin the by discussing visualization in general.

Visualization

As an athlete you are no doubt familiar with the term visualization. Often the term is defined as "recalling or forming mental images in your mind." That definition says nothing about directing or controlling the visualization process. I like the definition from The World English Dictionary, which defines visualization as "a technique involving focusing on positive mental images in order to achieve a particular goal." This definition better fits how visualization is discussed in this book since you select positive images (control) and focus on achieving a goal (direction of change).

You already do visualization, and you do it quite effectively. You think in images, not words. If you can't attach a symbol with meaning to a word, it has no meaning for you. For example, what are the meanings of the words mfwalashi and ngu'a. If you don't speak the languages, the words have no meaning. Now, if you can attach a picture of a horse to these words, they'll have meaning since each means horse, mfwalshi in Bemba and ngu'a in Vietnamese. Words only work when you attach images to them.

Dorfman and Kuehl, in their book *The Mental Game of Baseball,* describe the visualization process as "the ability to recall information in physical forms and images, instead of words." This definition broadens the term, moving beyond the visual (sight only) and bringing in the other physical senses such as sound, touch, kinesthetic feelings, taste, etc.

Researchers have found that when you incorporate these additional senses along with the visual, the visualization process is most powerful. The more senses used, the more powerful the visualization. Emotions are one of the most powerful sensations to add. If you can bring emotional feelings into your sessions, do so. This is illustrated by the formula I x V = R. Image times vividness equals reality.

$$I \times V = R$$
Image times Vividness equals Reality

To assist you in this, the worksheet in Appendix C will lead you through a recall event.

Although I've emphasized the importance of bringing in as much detail as possible, don't fret if you can't seem to get a detailed picture. Some people are called eidetic visualizers. This term refers to those who see everything clearly in bright, vivid colors. Most people are non-eidetic visualizers. This means you don't really see clear images but you just "think or imagine" them, or feel them kinesthetically.

Regardless of whether you are an eidetic or non-eidetic, visualization is one of the most powerful tools available to you as an athlete and it works for both types of visualizers. Along with the affirmations, visualization helps reset your reticular activating system (RAS) three different ways:

1. Visualizations, like affirmations, program the RAS to become aware of resources in your environment that can help you achieve your goals — resources you would not normally notice if your RAS was not activated to look for them. These may include people, books, audios and the like. Chances are they were always available, but you never noticed them before.

2. Visualization activates your subconscious mind to find creative solutions to achieve these visualized goals and behaviors. When you awake in the morning, throughout the day, and even when sleeping (dreaming), ideas, solutions and inspirations — those "aha" moments — often occur.

3. Visualization activates your success mechanism by motivating you to action, much like goals do. The more vivid the picture, the greater your enthusiasm. This helps you to step out of your current comfort zone and do things you haven't done in the past.

Mental Recall

Press the Rewind Button

Mental recall involves visualizing by reflecting back on previous successes and replaying these past experiences in your mind. For recall to be beneficial, the key is to focus on *successful* experiences. You've done recall all your life, but too often that recall is focused on what went wrong, and the reflecting is on a negative experience, sending the wrong images to your subconscious. Much like you control affirmations, you need to control the events you recall. Mental recall is like going into the video room and watching a successful at bat from yesterday, last week, last month or last year.

Recall incorporates two of the strongest principles of learning — (1) success breeds success and (2) repetition. You want to recall successful performances from the past to establish successful habits through repetition for the future.

Recall allows you to repeat past successes on a regular basis in your mind by replaying and reliving experiences in which you succeeded. And remember that main principle from Chapter 3, "Your body can't tell the difference between a real and an imagined experience!"

> *Think of a slump as a computer that's acting up. Sometimes it just needs to be rebooted. Recall, in a sense, reboots your mind to a time when it was set in a proper state for success.*

Each time you recall a successful experience, it is as if you are repeating that experience in the present. The more vividly you recall it, the more powerful the experience. This is most effective when you generate the corresponding emotions and feelings of success that you experienced during the original performance. One of the most effective ways to break out of a slump and regain confidence is by repeatedly recalling a time when you played at your best. Think of a slump as a computer that's acting up. Sometimes it just needs to be rebooted. Recall, in a sense, reboots your mind to a time when it was set in a proper state for success.

Performing mental recall on a regular basis is also a great way to stay in the flow state because you constantly replay positive experiences. Your subconscious mind knows you are successful because you've already succeeded.

Since the focus of this section of the book is on applying skills, let's move on immediately. I'll explain how to practice recall properly so that you get the most benefit from your time investment. Also, many of the suggestions in the next chapter on mental rehearsal will relate to mental recall, so I suggest you read both chapters so you have the best understanding of the processes before you begin incorporating them into your routine.

Guidelines for Successful Mental Recall

Select a Proper Experience

Since recall is designed to replay past successes, it is obvious that you want to be selective in what you recall. Go back to a time when you performed at your best or near best, both physically and mentally. Or recall a time when you played great in a pressure situation.

The experience you select doesn't have to be one where you were entirely successful — it could be an at bat where you got behind

Years ago I worked with Juan Nieves, then a young pitcher with the Milwaukee Brewers. I'd asked him to select a recall event from earlier in the year, to select a time when his confidence was at its high and he was really dealing on the mound. I assumed he would select an April game when he threw a no-hitter.

Following the exercise I led him through, I asked him to describe what he experienced. I was surprised to hear him say it was a different game. He explained that he threw well during the no hitter, but he was not at his best that day. The game he recalled was one where he gave up several runs, but it met the criteria for selecting a proper situation — when he was truly pitching effectively, was focused and attacked the strike zone with confidence and conviction. This was the day he felt he was at his best, not the night of the no hitter.

but relaxed, focused and had a key hit. In this instance, focus on the pitch you drove for the hit, not the previous pitches. Pitchers, you may have fallen behind 3-0 in the count with the bases loaded and then refocused, bore down, and got out of the jam.

Your Turn

List several potential recall events that come to mind:

1._____

2._____

3._____

Use as Much Detail as Possible to Reinforce Positive Feelings

After you've selected a recall experience, and before you practice it, go back and recall as many details about that day and that game as you can remember. Since success breeds success, you want to replicate much of what you experienced to solidify those feelings of success, confidence, joy and elation that you connect to that performance.

Use all of your senses and relive as much of the experience as you can, in as much detail as you can. Use sight, smell, sound, taste, temperature, emotional sensations, etc. The more you use, the more powerful the recall.

The most effective way to do this is to revisit the game you are recalling and make a list of all the things you can remember about the game itself as well as what you remember about the day. What you'll find is that when you do the recall, other experiences — ones you don't consciously remember — will pop up. These may be important to make the experience more powerful. Immediately after the recall, write down those additional things your subconscious remembered. That way the next time you recall that particular event you'll have even more detail to work into the experience.

Your Turn

In the space below each letter, A through C, write down as many details as possible of the game/experience you are recalling.

A. What experiences and sensations did you feel *prior* to that game? Those you may have experienced in the morning, afternoon, in the locker room, during BP, etc. Describe your level of confidence, your stress level, your emotions, your energy level, the weather, what your thoughts were, your goals, your expectations going to the park, etc. Make your list below, on a blank sheet, or go to Appendix C for a blank Mental Recall Worksheet or print off a copy of Appendix C at **baseballs6thtool.com**

_____

_____

_____

_____

_____

_____

_____

B. During the actual game (i.e., at bat, on the base path, making your pitch, fielding the ball, etc.), what did you experience? List what you felt in detail — your thoughts, emotions, stress level, kinesthetic feelings, confidence level, self-talk, body language and your senses (smell, sound, taste, temperature, sight). Use others if they spontaneously pop up during your awareness.

_____

_____

_____

_____

_____

_____

_____

C. Complete the picture. What did it feel like when you were standing on base or rounding the bases, walking back to the dugout after getting out of a challenging inning, or getting congratulated by coaches and teammates? How did you feel when you were interviewed after the game or when you looked at the box score?

_____

_____

_____

_____

_____

_____

You want to recall as many positive sensations, feelings, thoughts, and emotions as you possibly can. This worksheet will help you get started. After filling it out, review it before doing the recall to build a detailed picture in your mind of what you remember, then, when doing recall, allow your subconscious mind to take over and complete the picture.

Relive It from Inside Your Body

When visualizing, always view the experience from your own eyes, from within your body as if you are actually performing an at bat or making that pitch. When you visualize from within and feel the kinesthetic sensations, you reinforce the muscle memory in your neuromuscular system. Visualizing from within increases the chances of replicating those successful mechanics again in the future.

When you performed Chevreul's Pendulum earlier, you saw this in action. It illustrated several points regarding the mind-body connection. Your neuromuscular system responded to the image you placed in your mind. It works best when you are relaxed, and it *only* works when you visualize from within. Muscle memory patterns are not established when you see yourself performing on a screen — outside your body.

Use Actual Speed

Visualize at game speed. Only during full speed can your muscle memory benefit from the experience. The "kinesthetic feel" of a movement only reinforces the neuromuscular pattern at the speed imagined. Use game speed to maximize the muscle memory.

Carry Through to Completion

Generate any positive emotions related to the game you are recalling, and use them. Many emotions are experienced after the fact. You may want to recall events that took place after the game, such as the feeling of pride you had during an interview or the sense of accomplishment you felt as you read the box score the next morning. Recall being congratulated by coaches, teammates or a friend and replay what that felt like. Maybe you called someone after the game — a spouse, girl friend, or parent to talk about how you did. If, during the conversation, you experienced a feeling of pride, relive it.

Replay and recall all the positive feelings you can recapture that related to your performance. Feelings of confidence, happiness, success, contentment, pride and joy are all examples that make the recall more effective.

Your Turn

List below any emotions or positive feelings associated with the recall performance you selected that took place after the fact.

_____

_____

_____

_____

_____

_____

_____

Keep the Session Short

When working on your mental game, you want to be in a relaxed state physically and mentally, yet you want to remain alert. As discussed earlier in the relaxation chapter, one of the benefits of regular relaxation is improved focus and concentration. To get this benefit you must keep your mental focus while in the relaxed state. Keep your mind under control. Don't let it wander. Most sessions should be in the 3-5 minute range although when you use audios or hypnosis, they will be considerably longer.

Here are some things you can do if you get sleepy or your mind wanders:

1. Shorten the relaxation time so you don't get too relaxed. As long as you are in a relaxed, calm state, you are positioned for effective mental practice. Keep mental practice sessions in the 3-5 minute range.

2. Break up the session. If you get too relaxed, take a deep breath and open your eyes, close your eyes as you exhale, and then do the affirmations and recall.

Your Turn

It's time to practice mental recall in the relaxed state. Use a recall that you worked on in this chapter, and review the experiences you listed on your worksheet (A, B, and C on pages 121 and 122). Then, before you begin, read through the entire exercise below. When doing the recall, stick with one experience. Don't jump around to different games during the same session.

Recall Directions

1. Get in a comfortable position, either sitting or lying down.

2. Close your eyes, focus within, and feel yourself relaxing.

3. For a minute or two, relax using a relaxation technique you learned previously, i.e., as you exhale, and only when you exhale, focus on your body sinking down, slowing down, feeling heaviness and feeling warmth somewhere in your body. Just feel your body letting go of tension and relaxing.

4. Now recall the experience in detail (do so for 1-3 minutes, no more).

    a. What did you experience before?

    b. What did you experience during?

    c. What did you experience after?

5. When completed, take a deep breath as you stretch and open your eyes.

In sum...

- Mental recall activates your right brain — the creative portion — so that it works in conjunction with your left-brain, which is activated with the affirmations.

- Mental recall is like pressing the rewind button, going back in time and replaying successful experiences.

- Success breeds success. It's important to select proper recall experiences in which you recall positive outings.

- When done correctly, recall increases confidence and reinforces the proper muscle memory to replicate a movement, which contributes to better and more consistent performances.

- For maximum benefit, recall as many details as possible from within your body. Do not visualize yourself on a screen such as watching a video — see it from your own eyes.

- Since you are visualizing success and feeling, kinesthetically, the proper muscle movement where you played at your best, recall is one of the best techniques to use for slump busting.

CHAPTER 10

Mental Rehearsal

"Imagination is everything.
It is the preview of life's coming attractions."

Albert Einstein, Nobel Prize Winner

The previous chapter focused on the recall portion of visualization and emphasized the importance of replaying past successes in your mind. This chapter focuses on using visualization to create your future by picturing future performance. As Einstein said, imagination provides a preview of life's coming attractions.

To keep things in perspective, let's review so that you have a clear picture of the basic skills you employ to develop the mental game. The foundation is laid through evaluation and goal setting. This combination will paint a picture of where you are (evaluation) as well as where you want to go (goal setting). You use these processes to identify the gap between present and future and develop a plan to help you bridge that gap.

Next, you relax and place yourself in the calm, alpha state. This quiets your rational mind and increases the receptivity of your subconscious to suggestion. Then, through affirmations, you affirm (suggest) the behaviors you need to develop to move yourself toward your goals. This activates your left-brain, the logical portion. Next, you begin the visualization process with recall. This activates the right brain, the creative part of your brain, toward the same goals. With these skills at your disposal, you'll now add the fourth skill — mental rehearsal — that will continue the activation of the right brain and will also create the condition necessary to move your comfort zone to a higher level.

The mental recall portion of visualization prepares you for the upcoming rehearsal. Mental recall is like pushing the rewind button on your recorder and then replaying that experience. When you replayed the game in your mind, you felt not only what you experienced, but also the positive emotions associated with that experience. You now take these feelings associated with success and press the forward button, projecting these positive feelings and emotions to connect them to an imagined future performance. Rehearsal involves imagining future performances, perfectly executed in the variety of situations that you might encounter.

Mental Rehearsal Playing It Forward

How Mental Rehearsal Works

Although mental rehearsal provides the same benefits that recall provides, there is an additional major benefit that is critical in breaking out of your comfort zone. Again, since your body can't tell the difference between a real and an imagined experience, like recall, visualizing success increases confidence, and as you imagine correct mechanics from within your body, you lay down the proper muscle memory pattern. However, a third major benefit occurs with rehearsal that is not received when doing mental recall — it creates cognitive dissonance.

You mind cannot compute two conflicting thoughts without creating stress. When stress occurs, your mind must make adjustments to alleviate this stress and it does so by either (1) changing your behavior to be more in line with your thinking or (2) changing your thinking pattern. As you repetitively picture your new self, your mind creates this stress, and since you always move toward your dominate thoughts, the more often you imagine a brighter future, the more your subconscious mind begins to search for ways to move toward this new image. In other words, you get uncomfortable where you're at and your subconscious mind, to alleviate this stress, begins to identify behaviors that will move you from your current position to the new you.

Cognitive dissonance is a major factor in upping your comfort zone to a higher level. Unfortunately, it also works in reverse if you don't control the imagined images.

Just as recall done spontaneously often leads to recalling negative images, so too can spontaneous rehearsal lead to you visualizing negative situations, situations you want to avoid. These negative images cause stress, anxiety and worry about what the future might bring. Like you did with recall, you need to control the images you project so that you paint a picture of the future you desire.

Everyone has rehearsed — conjuring up a positive future. Some of you have already lived some of the things you've imagined in the past such as getting a scholarship, getting drafted, etc. Others events you may of lived on the field. Think back to when you were younger and playing whiffle ball in the yard. You come to the plate in the ninth inning of the World Series. Your team behind by two, two outs, the bases loaded . . . you get the idea. That's mental rehearsal. You hit it out of the park!

Successful rehearsal involves controlling and guiding your imagination so that you picture yourself achieving your goals and performing perfectly or near perfectly. In all successful rehearsal, you take ownership. You want to take control and guide the images because your future performance is at stake. Make that perfect pitch or make that game-winning hit — 100 percent of the time. This is probably the only time you should strive for perfection in a game setting (see Chapter 12 for more about perfectionism) since you have complete control over the pictures you place in your mind.

Mental rehearsal is a skill much like hitting, fielding, pitching, relaxing, affirming, recalling and concentrating. Like any skill, the more you practice, the better you get at it. It's a great skill to have at your disposal to etch the image of a positive future onto your subconscious mind. Since you always move toward your dominant thoughts, make these thoughts successful thoughts.

Benefits of Mental Rehearsal

As stated earlier, mental rehearsal is one of the most powerful tools you have at your disposal in creating your future. Done properly, it can bring enormous benefits likes those listed below.

Rehearsal increases your self-image and confidence.

Since you always perform consistently with your self-image, you want to strengthen your self-image to elevate your success zone. Rehearsal involves the same principle as recall; your body can't tell the difference between a real experience and an imagined one. When you picture a successful future — such as striding to the plate with a confident swagger or standing tall and confident on the mound — your subconscious accepts this as a true image. You respond with accompanying positive emotions and feel confident, strong and powerful. If, on the other hand, you fear the future, the pictures you created in your mind actually cause stress and corresponding negative emotions. What better reason to stay positive!

You can rehearse for all future situations you may encounter.

Preparing for various situations is one of the greatest benefits of rehearsal. You no doubt have projected yourself into the future and imagined being at the plate or on the mound at a critical time in a game. Do the same thing now, and then picture yourself performing exactly as you want. You can be successful 100 percent of the time. This is a great way to use rehearsal.

Every time you rehearse your future, you are laying the foundation for success and greater consistency when you encounter similar situations. When you're in a game, and you find yourself in a situation you've rehearsed, you've already been through that experience and performed successfully — thousands of times if you rehearsed it often enough. This familiarity with the situation and knowing you have successfully navigated it allows you to face it more confidently, more relaxed, and more focused than if it was new and completely unknown. The more often you project and succeed in your mind, the more prepared you'll be when you experience it in real life.

Rehearsal reinforces a positive neuromuscular blueprint.

Like recall, whenever you visualize a physical skill, your body responds subliminally by activating your muscular and nervous system to fire in the same sequence as if you were actually performing that skill. That's why it is so important to always visualize success. Visualizing failure lays the foundation for failure no matter how badly you want success or how hard you work physically.

Rehearsal helps reduce stress.

Whenever you visualize a successful future, you take some of the uncertainty out of it, which means a lower stress level. You feel more in control of your future, and anytime you feel in control, your confidence level is elevated. Likewise, when you feel things are out of your control, doubt enters and confidence wavers.

The How To of Successful Mental Rehearsal

Mental rehearsal uses guidelines similar to those of mental recall, with a few slight variations. The details explained below can also be adapted to make your mental recall more effective. Be flexible, and adapt by personalizing your rehearsal.

Develop the Proper Scenario

In recall, you selected a time when you performed at or near your best physically. In rehearsal, you create a performance in your mind in which you do play at your best. This is one of the greatest benefits of rehearsal. You can bat .1000, and you can pitch the perfect game. If you look at Paul Molitor's experience of batting .1000 in his mind (pages 171-172), you can see how your body responds.

Research has shown that visualization can be as effective — perhaps even more effective — than physical practice because of your opportunity to play it perfectly. If you overdo physical practice, you often practice poor mechanics due to mental or physical fatigue. Rehearsal allows you to "practice perfect."

Use as Much Detail as Possible

Incorporate as many senses as possible into your rehearsal. For example, imagine yourself in a specific stadium — it could be your home stadium or an away stadium — the stands are full. Picture your teammates and coaches before, during, and after the game. See the stadium, the field and the locker room. Feel the cold or warmth of the weather, or maybe the wind blowing. The more detail you include in your mind's eye, the more powerful the imagery.

What do you hear? Can you hear the crowd noise? How about a vendor in the stands between innings? Maybe fans shouting support when at home or fans riding you in an away stadium.

What do you smell? Can you smell the freshness of a spring day? Smelling the various aromas of the concession stands such as popcorn, the grilling burgers or brats. How about freshly cut grass?

You can even incorporate the sense of touch. What do you feel? Maybe it's the material of your clothes against your skin. Maybe it's drizzling during the game, so you may be feeling damp, cold or even miserable.

What do you taste? This may be less important than the other senses, but it also could be a key sense to complete the picture. An example may be the salty taste of sweat on your upper lip. It might be a refreshing beverage between innings or the taste of champagne as it's being poured over your head as you celebrate a championship.

You get the idea. Don't hold back. Let your mind go to work and begin creating a mental movie of your future.

> **Have in mind the great image, and the empire will come to you.**
>
> LAO-TSE, TAO TE CHING

Place yourself in situations you may encounter in the future.

This is one of the greatest benefits of using rehearsal. You can place yourself in any imaginable situation and picture yourself succeeding. Whenever you encounter a similar situation, you will be better prepared. You will have increased your chances of success because in your mind you've been there, rose to the occasion and navigated the situation successfully.

You may want to place yourself at bat or on the mound with the winning run on second in a playoff game or the World Series. The outcome of the game is on your shoulders and millions are watching on TV. Feel the adrenalin, the stress, even the shaky knees. Then visualize going through your routine, going to the perfect tension level, feeling relaxed, focused, confident — and dominating.

Bring in rotten weather. The season starts in April and the World Series is played in late October and early November. With that in mind, you may want to imagine that you love cold weather. Train your mind so it is prepared for inclement weather. Perhaps you could even imagine enjoying the cold or snow, knowing it doesn't affect you but it *devastates* your opponent. You could imagine the opposite as well.

Imagine playing for the fourth straight day in 100-degree tempera-tures. You feel the sweat roll off of your body — and you overcome the conditions. You've developed a mental edge, and you perform at your best in spite of the elements.

Years ago when I was in college, a coach once scolded our team when he heard players complaining about the weather. He said, "There's is no such thing as bad weather, just soft people." So incorpo-rate various weather conditions in your rehearsal, and toughen up. Get ready for the cold days of April and October as well as the sweltering days of summer. Remember the self-filling prophecy? If you expect to feel exhausted or uncomfortable, you will! So change your expecta-tions, and prepare with rehearsal.

Relive It from Inside Your Body, Using Actual Speed

Like recall, you want to experience the rehearsal from within your body and using actual speed to gain the greatest benefits. As you perform perfectly in your mind, you establish the neuromuscular blueprint in your body. This increases your chance of replicating the imagined performance in the future.

Carry it through to completion.

This is the fun part of visualization. You get to rehearse every-thing from start to finish, and you get to imagine what it would be like to get that game-winning hit in the World Series, throw the perfect game, pile on your teammates after the last out, celebrate in the locker room, experience the powerful emotions later by celebrating with loved ones.

That's the power of your mind. During rehearsal, you are the screenwriter, the director and the main character. The script is always a great script, one with a perfect ending. And you get to experience all of the accompanying positive emotions and anchor these emotions and experiences into your mind.

Vary mental rehearsal.

Another benefit of mental rehearsal is that you can vary how and when you project your future. You can use it every day to rehearse your upcoming practices. Select a main goal or theme for your next infield, batting practice or bullpen, then, before practice, rehearse the skills you will work on during that session. This is a great way to get the most out of practice because you come in prepared and have a goal for each activity.

Your Turn

Create your future.

Develop a scenario in your mind before performing the following exercise. Be sure to read through the entire technique before you do it the first time. Although both mental recall and mental rehearsal are often used together in the same exercise, for simplicity's sake this exercise will include just the relaxation and the rehearsal skills. Other combinations will be illustrated in Chapter 11.

1. Get into a comfortable position, either sitting or lying down.

2. Close your eyes, focus within, and feel your body relaxing.

3. For a moment or two, focus on your exhalations, and relax as you exhale. Focus on your body sinking down, slowing down, and feeling heavy and warm over a 2-3 minute period. Take your time, exhale, relax and let go of all tension.

4. Now, go into the scene you imagined, and develop the scenario in your mind.

    a. Be part of the scene. See, hear, and feel being in the scene.

    b. Then picture yourself at bat, in the field or on the mound.

    c. If you're a position player, take a minute or two picturing a future game and having a perfect at bat. Lay off pitches out of your zone while driving those in your zone for hits. Use different situations. Face different pitchers as you prepare for future success. Practice plate discipline.

    d. If you're a pitcher, take a minute or two and picture a future outing, pitching accurately, locating all of your pitches, getting the desired result such as a strike out or a ground ball. Imagine a variety of batters you'll face in the future, applying and being successful in implementing your game plan. Attack the strike zone with complete confidence and conviction.

5. When done, simultaneously flex, stretch, and open your eyes just like you would when you wake up in the morning.

In sum…

- Mental rehearsal is the fourth of the foundation skills of a mental skills program.

- Its benefits include increasing confidence, reinforcing proper muscle memory and creating cognitive dissonance (stress) in your mind, which is critical in breaking out of your comfort zone.

- Cognitive dissonance forces your subconscious to search for ways to elevate your performance because your subconscious always seeks balance, and two conflicting thoughts create unbalance.

- It's of critical importance for you to imagine the correct results so you move in that direction. If you imagine negative behaviors and results, you can just as easily move the wrong way. Control your rehearsal!

- Rehearsal, like all skills, can be improved with practice.

PART 4

Applying the
Mental Game

As stated in the introduction, your goal is not to learn a program but to change behaviors so you perform at a higher level consistently. You've been introduced to the mental skills that, when used properly, change behavior. Now is the time to apply these skills.

In this part of the book, we'll focus on applying the concepts to common situations and challenges you may encounter on your journey. Chapter 11 provides suggestions that will make implementation of the program more successful. In this chapter you will learn two ways to apply the four basic mental skills.

Chapters 12, 13 and 14 will discuss several challenges most players are confronted with during their career. Each chapter will provide suggestions on how to overcome these challenges with your mental skills program. Chapter 12 deals with confidence, which at the onset was described as the most important ingredient required to play at a high level more consistently. Chapter 13 focuses on concentration, and I review several techniques you can use to increase your ability in this area. Finally, in Chapter 14, you will find suggestions on how to use your mind to speed up the healing process following injuries.

CHAPTER 11

Making It Yours

"We all have a similar story, we're just different characters. We all travel the same route, we just see different scenery."

Unknown

Great things happen only when you develop the proper strategy and then apply it. They only happen on purpose, rarely by chance. This chapter will discuss ways to implement a strategy successfully so you have a program that works for you.

In the introduction I compared the mental game to a jigsaw puzzle. I stated that as you move through the various chapters, you may not at first understand how all the parts fit together, but by the end of the book, the picture on the puzzle box will begin to take shape. If you've made it this far and worked through the exercises, you should have a good idea of the importance of the mental game and how to make it work for you. Now to complete the puzzle, you will need the final piece — learning how to successfully implement what you've learned.

As the opening quote to this chapter states, we all have a similar story. Your trip up to and around the major leagues will take a route similar to most other players, but the scenery you see and the challenges you must overcome to reach your goals will be different from what others experience. Likewise as you read this book, you will discover that what you experienced — the thoughts, the insight and the inspirations you may have — are vastly different from the experiences of others reading the same material.

Keep this in mind as you develop *your* mental game plan. No two programs will look alike — yours *will* and *should* be unique and personal to you.

Considerations in putting your plan together should include:

• Where *you* are today.

• *Your* goals for the future.

• The program *you* design to close the gap between the two.

• *Your* family commitments.

• *Your* time restraints.

• How much time *you* are willing to commit to it, etc.

These and many other considerations will determine the program that works best for you. I've found that those players who most effectively apply their inner game tend to keep it simple, practical and flexible so that they do it routinely. Keep these thoughts in mind as you develop your game plan.

Let's go back to the jigsaw puzzle analogy. The puzzle is composed of many pieces, and at the start it is difficult to see how they all fit together. To complete the picture, you will need a large solid surface to assemble it on. The four legs supporting that foundation are the four basic mental skills — relaxation, affirmations, mental recall and mental rehearsal. It's important to master all four foundation skills so that you activate your entire brain for success. How each piece of the puzzle is used — when, how you adapt them, the order in which you apply them — will differ from how another player might use them.

The foundational skills are basic to behavior change. When I work individually with players, we go into much more depth than what is being presented in this book. There are a myriad of other concepts and skills not discussed here that are critical to success on the field. These four basic skills lay the foundation to change your inner self, your self-image. Without making this interior change, you are doomed to repeat past mistakes, and you will always drift back to your old comfort zone regardless of your mechanics or other auxiliary skills you have learned, such as focusing, relaxing, developing a routine etc.

Suggestions for Implementing a Successful Program

Although each player will develop a program unique to him, the following provides some suggestions that will help you successfully apply your program.

1. Practice daily. To succeed with your mental plan, you must apply it in the same manner as your physical plan. Practice daily so that self-talk, beliefs, attitudes, and behaviors are positive and as automatic as your swing or pitching mechanics. Becoming the new you, both on and off the field, will only happen quickly and permanently if you commit to it. If a goal is truly important to you, you should work on it daily. This includes your mental skills goal, which should be one of the most important goals for your future, if not the most important.

2. Develop a routine. One of the reasons players get away from daily practice is they don't build it into their routine. Schedule it into your day at a regular time each and every day. I suggest connecting your practice session to current daily routines. As mentioned previously, a good time to begin is in the morning upon waking because you are in a receptive state. The same holds true in the evening. Other times may be just before you go to the park, during down time at the park, after BP, or following your daily workout. Connecting it to a routine already established, such as before or after you read the paper or after the news, will help you make it a habit.

3. Be flexible. The program you develop must work for you. Remember, the goal is not to do a program, it's to change

behavior. If one approach you try doesn't work, adapt it, add to it, delete from it, etc. Your routine is not carved in granite — it can be altered.

For many players, I alter their program regularly to keep it fresh. Like anything else, too much repetition can get boring. Don't let things get stale or they lose their effectiveness.

4. Practice what you preach. Make it one of your goals to work on your mental skills daily. Then use the same steps to reinforce this goal. Relax, affirm it, recall a time when you've successfully followed a routine in the past, and see yourself practicing mental skills daily.

5. Log it. As emphasized throughout this book, you want to utilize everything at your disposal to increase your chances of success. Research has shown that when you log or journal behaviors on a daily basis, you increase your chances of making a successful change. Use a simple notebook, log or journal. Design your log to fit your needs. Again, there is no correct way to log. The correct way is one that works for you.

Sample Programs

I'd like to lay out a couple of sample programs to illustrate how you can implement a daily routine with little time investment. I use the term "investment" because it implies a return greater than what you started with. If you invest your money, you expect more back from that investment. The term "time investment" as used here means you can expect greater returns — 10 fold, 20 fold or more for the time you commit to your mental skills practice.

Both programs are presented to provide you with ideas you may use or adapt. Both use the four basic skills, but the way in which they are applied differs. In the first sample discussed, there is a greater emphasis on the relaxation, and the affirmation portion focuses on a specific trait or behavior. In this program, you will use only short, one-sentence affirmations. Next you will add the mental recall of when you exhibited that trait, followed by rehearsal, in which you visualize yourself in the future displaying the desired trait or performing at your best.

In the second program presented, you can either relax and/or get comfortable and calm to make your mind more receptive. This approach focuses on the affirmation. The affirmation can be specific or more detailed, describing a combination of behaviors or traits. You then contemplate or reflect on the trait(s), or visualize being that person and displaying the trait today and/or in the future. The rehearsal or reflection portion of this approach is only 20-40 seconds.

The programs are similar because they both use the foundations steps for changing behaviors. Many of the players I work with use one of the two, but most end up incorporating parts of each, adapting them to their individual routines. Some go back and forth from one style to the other.

You can mix and match, use one or the other, or develop a plan completely different from these two. Just make it a plan you can stick with and do routinely.

Sample Program 1
The Mindset for Winning Program (MFW)

The Mindset for Winning program illustrates how you can use the steps in a logical sequence. I've used this approach successfully with athletes for more than 30 years and published it originally in 1987 in the book *The Mindset for Winning: A Four-Step Mental Training Program for Athletes.* I've adapted it specifically to baseball, and new audio programs are available for both pitchers and position players (English and Spanish versions) at **baseballs6thtool.com**. These downloads can assist you in learning the four basic steps.

Although the book was first published almost 25 years ago, the basic principles are principles of nature and, like gravity, have not changed. The MFW program is just as effective today as it was when first published. In the program, you simply implement the four foundation steps on a daily basis, usually 2 or 3 times a day for 3 to 4 minutes each session.

Preparation

Before you begin the four steps, you should have done your evaluation and written out your goals. Next you will identify the behaviors you want to change or strengthen to accomplish these goals. Again, emphasize the behavior you want to exhibit, not avoid.

For simplicity's sake I'll outline a simple program using the MFW model. Develop a short affirmation based on your goal. Remember, in this model you want the affirmation to be short and direct. Here are several examples.

"I am confident and relaxed."

"I am quick and aggressive in my zone."

"I am calm, relaxed and patient at the plate."

"Through the grace of God, I can do it."

Your Turn

Affirmation: Write a short affirmation on a trait you display when playing at your best.

_____

_____

_____

_____

Now follow these directions and do an entire MFW session using all four steps. Be sure to read all directions before beginning.

1. Relax: Using one of the techniques involving breathing, spend 1-2 minutes relaxing until you feel calm and relaxed and focused.

2. Affirmation: Each time you exhale (and *only* as you exhale) repeat the short affirmation to yourself. Do this for 5-6 breaths, one time per exhalation.

3. Recall: Visualize a time in the past when you exhibited this characteristic. It could be a game, an inning or maybe just one pitch. Recall it in detail and remember how you felt and what you experienced. Do this for a minute or so.

4. Rehearsal: Take the feeling you had during your successful recall and visualize yourself performing in the future as you display that characteristic in a game setting. See yourself actually being that person and achieving the results you want. Do this for a minute or so.

5. When done, take a deep breath and simultaneously flex, stretch and open your eyes.

There you have it. It's quick, simple and powerful when done on a regular basis. Do it three times a day, such as in the morning, mid-day, and in the evening or at other scheduled, routine times.

Suggestions that May Help You Do the MFW Model

As you get better with relaxation, you can cut the time you spend getting into the alpha state because you'll be getting there more quickly. Early on, a session may take 5-7 minutes because you are learning to relax. Once you've learned how, you should be able to relax in 1 minute or even in 2-3 breaths when you get good at it. At this level, you can spend more time on the affirmations and the imagery, and you will then be able to bring your sessions down to the 3-5 minute timeframe.

You can vary your daily routine by using different relaxation techniques, different affirmations, different recall events, and you should picture yourself in a variety of situations where you successfully perform and display the traits you want to manifest. In the rehearsal step, be sure to place yourself under stressful conditions. Imagine a situation where you struggled in the past, then visualize meeting that challenge and being successful in that situation. You may want to imagine the playoffs or the World Series and visualize succeeding in those environments.

Sample Program 2

Affirmation-Based Program

The second program illustrates how to use the four basic components in a slightly different version. For many years I was locked into the MFW model until I met Frank Bartenetti, a man who was a "success coach" before there was such a term. Frank introduced me to this version, which uses affirmations as the focal point. It is based on Lou Tice's Pacific Institute program. For many years Frank was vice president of the Pacific Institute, and in that role he worked with highly successful business men and women from around the world.

Frank also worked with athletes from a variety of sports and at all levels of accomplishment. Kirk Gibson, current manager for the Arizona Diamondbacks, in his book titled *The Bottom of the Ninth,* discusses Frank's impact on his career. After spending two days with Frank when he was only 22, Kirk was able to develop from a struggling player to a successful professional who was an NL MVP and was on two World Series Championship teams. He may be best known for his 1988 World Series home run against Oakland in his only at bat during that series due to injuries and illness.

Preparation

In this version you can use multiple, more lengthy affirmations. For example, if you're a position player, you may want to work on being quick and powerful in your swing, being more confident and seeing the ball out of the pitcher's hand. A pitcher may want to affirm standing tall, getting on top of the ball and attacking the strike zone down and in. Both examples illustrate how you can combine several behaviors into one affirmation. You can go either way, develop four different affirmations or develop one or two more lengthy ones as illustrated in the affirmation chapter. Get your affirmations together, and then find a quiet place to sit down and do the following exercise.

Your Turn

1. Get in a comfortable position, close your eyes, and in 1 or 2 breaths relax or just place yourself into a state of calmness.

2. Open your eyes and read the first affirmation.

3. Close your eyes and reflect on, contemplate or visualize — for 20 to 40 seconds — becoming that person and displaying the trait you are affirming.

4. Open your eyes and read the second affirmation.

5. Close your eyes and repeat step three above.

6. Continue doing the same with each affirmation.

7. When done, open your eyes and go about your day.

In this model you will do your session and then just go about your ordinary day. You don't need to change anything. When your subconscious is ready to change, it will remind you to display the new behaviors, and eventually you will begin to display them by habit. Remember, permanent change comes from within and always works its way out.

I particularly like this approach because it allows you to work on multiple traits at the same time with little time investment. The results often occur incredibly quickly.

I found the most effective way to apply this approach is to put each affirmation on a 3" x 5" card. I often laminate them for durability. Using index cards provides more flexibility. Once you begin to display the characteristics, you replace the original affirmation(s) with new ones. You can use the older affirmations once or twice a week to reinforce them. This way you to keep reinforcing the behaviors you've changed over a longer period. It's important to reinforce these new behaviors occasionally so you don't drift back to the old habits.

Audio Programs

Another way to implement these steps is by listening to audio programs currently available. Audios can be very effective in learning and reinforcing various skills and behaviors.

At our website, **baseballs6thtool.com,** a variety of audio programs are available for download. These programs are designed around the most common topics and behaviors confronted by players. When I work individually with a player I often make a personalized audio specifically designed around that player's needs. Obviously a program that has been individualized for you would be the most effective.

Hypnosis

Hypnosis is another approach used to apply the four basic skills. You've probably been introduced to hypnosis by seeing "stage hypnotists." If this is your idea of hypnosis, you may have a distorted, negative view of the art. Let me assure you that what you see with a stage hypnotist is not how it is applied in sports. Hypnosis can be a very successful tool in changing behaviors and improving performances.

I use hypnosis with approximately 10-15 percent of the players I work with. Most players can achieve the same benefits with a well-rounded mental skills program. I've found hypnosis to be most effective for the following circumstances:

1. Identifying the root cause of a negative behavior and using it to eliminate that cause.

2. Jump starting change, especially with athletes who want an immediate change. For example, a player who is dealing with an extended slump during the season needs immediate help. Hypnosis can provide that immediate infusion of confidence to help him get over the hump.

3. Dealing with negative behavior traits that may be affecting performance or even a career if not changed. The more ingrained the negative habit, the greater the need for imme-

diate relief, and with hypnosis change begins almost imme-diately. Behavioral issues and extreme negativism, throwing issues, etc., are examples.

When I use hypnosis, I combine it with a mental skills program as a follow-up. You need daily practice to reinforce the change to make it permanent. Without this reinforcement, it is easy to revert to previous behavior patterns over time.

Again, at our website, **baseballs6thtool.com**, self-hypnosis tapes are available to help you to develop and reinforce new behaviors.

Hypnosis works slightly differently than using the four basic steps for change. In the programs presented in this book, your conscious mind determines what is to be done (ideas), and the four steps systematically impress this new image on the sub-conscious, which furnishes the power to make the change.

Under hypnosis, you go into a much deeper state. While in this trance-like state, the conscious mind turns control of the input (ideas) over to the hypnotist for the time being. The hyp-notist thus becomes the originator of ideas and presents them to the subconscious to carry out. Remember, the subconscious is the "goal seeker" and has no power to reject, analyze, judge or disagree with the ideas it is given. The deeper the state, the more likely it will accept these new thoughts as fact, and the subcon-scious acts on anything it accepts as true. Hypnosis most often takes place at theta level of consciousness, which is usually deeper than you place yourself during relaxation (see Figure 7-1).

In sum...

- A successful program is one you personalize. It should be a program that works for you.

- Success in your mental game requires the same dedication as that toward your physical game. Develop a routine that works, practice daily, and log or journal daily to increase your chances for success.

- Remember to keep your program simple. The programs explained allows you to incorporate the four foundation steps in a simple 2–7 minute session.

CHAPTER 12

Confidence

"Confidence is preparation.
Everything else is beyond your control."

Richard Kline

"When there is no enemy within,
the enemies outside cannot hurt you."

African Proverb

Confidence is the key to consistent performance. Think of confidence as the feeling of knowing you are always up to the task
at hand. When your confidence is high, you approach situations with
100 percent conviction. The biggest confidence booster of all is preparation.

One day during batting practice, I was in the outfield speaking with pitcher Miguel Batista, who has appeared in more than 600
games spanning a 17-year career in the major leagues. We were discussing the relationship between confidence and performance. He
told me that when he was 100 percent prepared, both physically and
mentally, he could take the mound with complete confidence and
pitch with total conviction. However, if he was only 99 percent prepared in either area, there was that little voice of doubt in the back
of his mind that affected his pitching. Total confidence comes from
complete preparation, both physical and mental.

Environments and situations may vary, and your confidence can
fluctuate as well. You may be very confident at the plate or on the
mound, yet your confidence plummets in other situations, such as
speaking in front of a group or taking a leadership role. Your confi-

dence may be high in conversations with teammates, yet it's much lower when trying to express yourself to a coach. Your level of confidence in different situations during a game also varies. You may be more confident defensively than at the plate or on the mound. A pitcher may be more confident in his slider than his change-up.

Great ballplayers have an unshakable confidence and inner belief in themselves and their skills on the field. Hall-of-Famer Ty Cobb illustrated this inner confidence during an interview late in his life.

When [Cobb] was 70 years old, a reporter inquired, "What do you think you'd hit if you were playing these days?"

Cobb, who had a lifetime average of .367 said, "About .290 or maybe .300."

Next the reporter asked, "Is that because of the travel, the night games, the artificial turf, and all the new pitches like the slider?"

"No," said Cobb. "It's because I'm 70 years old."

Now that's the level of confidence you want in your abilities!

Confidence Drives Performance

Consistency and confidence go hand in hand. You'll never play consistently at a high level unless you develop an unshakable, high degree of confidence in your abilities. Players with a high degree of inner confidence approach their mental game much like their physical game — they work at it. They either consciously or subconsciously engage in activities that strengthen their inner beliefs. They have developed habitual ways of thinking that work for them regardless of the results.

As you know, baseball is a humbling game, and it can quickly erode confidence. You need to work at maintaining your belief in yourself. The remainder of this chapter will cover several mindsets that are most detrimental to confidence, and it will provide examples of how to readjust that mindset. Again, this is not all-inclusive but will provide you examples of how you can approach various issues.

The Detrimental Mindset: The Negative Player

Nothing is more detrimental than a negative mindset. Those with a negative mindset often take on the role of the victim. *Everything* seems to go against them, and they can find something negative about any situation.

When I've worked with negative players, they've actually told me, "It's just the way I am," and "I can't do anything about it," or "I was born like this." What a great way to relinquish control! Imagine the shock on your mother's face when the doctor held you up after birth, slapped your butt, and said, "We've got a negative one here!"

During a meeting with a major league player, I told him he had the most negative mindset I'd ever seen in a player — and he actually went out and bragged about it to his teammates and coaches. He was comfortable as a major league bench player. He wanted to play better, but he didn't want to work on changing his negative thinking.

One of my favorite movie scenes is in the Jim Carey film "Liar, Liar." If you've seen the film, you will recall the scene where he goes into the men's room and physically beats himself up. If you haven't seen this film, you should check it out tonight. He's doing *physically* exactly what negative people do *mentally*. They beat themselves to a pulp. It's not logical; it doesn't make any sense to think you can improve performance by beating yourself down with negative thoughts.

Perfectionism

One of the major contributors to a negative mindset is perfectionism. Perfectionism is the enemy of greatness. You can't be great if you think you have to play perfectly because every time you fail, you tell yourself you'll never be perfect — and you're right. The biggest cause of a negative mindset is falling into the trap of perfectionism. Of all the players I've worked with, the ones I'd classify as having the most negative mindsets have nearly all described themselves as being perfectionists.

The problem with thinking you have to play perfectly or you're a failure is that you can't be perfect, especially in the game of baseball. As you've been told repeatedly, baseball is a game of failure. While your conscious mind recognizes that nobody is perfect, if you've got the perfectionist mindset, your subconscious believes you have to be perfect — and anytime you perform less than that (which is most always), your self-talk pulls you toward the negative cycle described in Chapter 2, thus hindering consistent performance.

Perfectionists continually berate themselves mentally. This is not only discouraging, but it also lowers your self-esteem and saps energy. Perfectionists are continually frustrated — and so are the teammates who have to listen to all the bullshit and whining. And the negative cycle continues.

Reframe your thinking so that you strive for excellence, not perfection. Be the best you can be today. Striving for excellence is stimulating and rewarding, while striving for perfection is frustrating and futile.

Breaking the Cycle of Negativity

Everyone has negative thoughts. Research has shown that 77 percent of the average person's thoughts are negative. So regardless of how well you are playing and how positive you are, negative thoughts will creep in. This is especially true when things aren't going well. Controlling these thoughts is the key. When you notice them, immediately take control and change them so that the negative cycle doesn't get established. If you find that you've been negative, you may be surprised to learn that it is quite easy to break the cycle and get back on a positive track — regardless of how long you've been in this mindset. The only requirement is that you must choose to change.

To begin this change, you need to reframe your thinking on a conscious level. Struggles are opportunities to illustrate to coaches and others how you respond to challenges. Your goal should be to grow bigger than your problems. It's been said that you should "thank God for problems — they're opportunities to grow and become prepared for a larger stage." If you're struggling where you're at, that's a good indication that you've got something to learn before you move to the next level. Learn now, and you'll be better prepared for opportunities when the proper time comes.

John Wooden, legendary UCLA basketball coach, stated, "Condition yourself to love the struggle. It's just a matter of time." This is a great way to reframe your view of struggles. Love them, embrace them, and don't shy away from them — outgrow them! Along this same line of thinking, J. William Marriott said, "Good timber does not grow with ease. The stronger the wind, the stronger the trees." So view struggles from a different view-

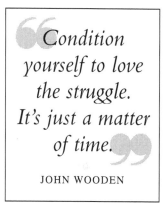

Condition yourself to love the struggle. It's just a matter of time.

JOHN WOODEN

point, a more positive light. They are challenges and opportunities for growth and change.

Revamping Negative Thinking

There is a very quick and easy way to revamp negative think-ing. You simply reset your RAS to search for positive things rather than negative things. Negative people have, over time, set their RAS for negativity without intending to do so. You need to reset it — in-tentionally. The results not only happen quickly, but can benefit your game tremendously.

An example of how quickly thinking can be turned from nega-tive to positive, with the resulting change in performance, is described in the side story titled "Jamie McOwen: 45-Game Hitting Streak." Jamie graciously allowed me to share this story with you. He used the gratitude journal to reset his RAS, and the result was immediate — he began to play up to his potential consistently.

Jamie Mc Owen: 45-Game Hitting Streak

Jamie's story of his 45-game hitting streak illustrates two points: the significant difference a very little change can make in performance, and the power of the gratitude journal.

In May 2009 I made a trip to visit the High Desert Mavericks, at that time an advanced-A ball affiliate for the Seattle Mariners. My last day there, May 14th, Jamie asked to meet. He was frustrated, batting .269 at the time, just above his two-year minor league average of .260.

Jamie was a perfectionist, and like most perfectionists, he was always beating himself up mentally. Since I was leaving that day and we had little time together, he'd decided to work on the negativity that comes with perfectionism. His task was to begin a gratitude journal and email me a copy each day for a week, but to continue doing the journal after that.

On the day we met Jamie had already hit safely in three games. He continued hitting safely for a total of 45 games, the longest minor league hitting streak in 55 years. He shattered the California league record of 36 games. He raised his average to .355, hitting .398 during the streak itself.

I only met with Jamie that day for 30 minutes, and my only role was to give him a copy of "How to Do a Gratitude Journal." Jamie took it from there and worked the journal diligently. He had a historic run, illustrating the power of a positive mindset and how it relates to consistent performance. I met with Jamie after the season and he shared how his mindset had changed and how this new mindset contributed largely to his streak.

Note: Unfortunately, in April 2010, after being promoted to AA, Jamie crashed into a wall during a game and separated his shoulder for the third time, an injury that required season-ending surgery.

Your Turn

Using a Gratitude Journal to Reset Your RAS

A gratitude journal is designed to help you refocus your mind onto positive thoughts. It is a quick and easy way to revamp a negative mindset and turn it into a positive one. We've all had many blessings in our lives that either we no longer recognize as blessings or we've started to take for granted. The objective of a gratitude journal is to reset your RAS to search for all of the blessings and to recognize the abundance we have in our lives, to look for things we have forgotten or assume we will have forever. A negative mindset is geared toward looking for problems, not blessings. Once you begin to search for blessings, your RAS is reset and the result is often immediate and profound.

Directions for Using a Gratitude Journal

1. Get a notebook and title it "Gratitude Journal." This is an important step, and if you skip it your chances of successful change will be diminished.

2. Each evening before going to bed, review your day's activities and write down all the things that went well for you that day. Nothing is too insignificant. Anything that went right should be noted. Some examples may be something as simple as noticing what a great day it was, a positive conversation with a friend or loved one, a beautiful sunset, a refreshing drink when hot, a restful nap, feeling good after cleaning the house, a good meal or feeling healthy.

   The goal of this journal is to look for things that are right in your life — not things that are going wrong. You're not looking for winning the lottery. You're looking for the simple things in life that you take for granted so that you begin to have a renewed sense of how fortunate and blessed you are.

3. Each evening, number the things on your list that you not-
    ed for that day. Each day your list should be growing larger.
    You'll begin to recognize more positive things — even on
    days that may not be great.

4. You will notice that some things get repeated each day.
    That's not only okay, it is desirable. Write them down each
    day. Things like a loving family, a positive phone call home
    after a game, maid-service at the hotel, a great peanut butter
    sandwich in the locker room (just kidding) might appear
    daily.

5. Each morning review the previous day's listings and set a
    goal of coming up with a larger number that day than the
    previous day.

Using the Affirmation/Reflection Process

Use the affirmation/reflection approach in addition to the
gratitude journal. An affirmation may be as simple as "I am always
positive, and I search for blessing every day." Or use an affirmation
to reinforce your goal of doing the gratitude journal, such as, "Each
evening I write in my gratitude journal, and every morning I review
it. I am grateful for the blessings I receive each day."

Change Your Self-Talk

Once you establish the goal of becoming more positive and begin the gratitude journal and affirmations, you will become aware
of negative thoughts and actions when they occur. This is your RAS
working toward your new goal. When negative thoughts occur, immediately stop the behavior and rephrase your self-talk. For example,
after you notice a negative thought, say "Cancel!" or "Stop — that's
NOT me! I am positive, and I always focus on the positive," or something similar.

In sum...

- Self-confidence and consistently high performances go hand in hand. The greater your confidence, the better and more consistent your performance.

- The biggest deterrent to being confident is negative self-talk, which most often creeps in without conscious thought. Berating yourself will not improve performance, it will only hinder it.

- Perfectionism is a major contributor to negative self-talk, which has a detrimental effect on performance. Remember, perfectionism is the enemy of greatness.

- There are several easy and effective approaches to reset your RAS and change your outlook from a negative to positive.

- As with everything else, you must choose to change and then apply an effective strategy to bring about the change.

CHAPTER 13

Improving Concentration: You Must Be *Present* to Win

"Clear the mechanism."

Kevin Costner, "For the Love of the Game"

One of my favorite baseball movies is "For the Love of the Game" starring Kevin Costner. If you've seen the movie, you probably recall the scene where he takes the mound in a crucial game. The visual effect of Costner's concentration moving from a soft to a hard focus and the graphic intensity he exhibits illustrates the power of the affirmation "Clear the Mechanism." The end result is total concentration on the glove. There are absolutely no other thoughts or distractions. What a great skill to have!

I often have coaches tell me that a particular player just can't focus or that he loses his concentration during games. I hear this same thing from players, who admit they have difficulty focusing or turning their minds off.

We all have the ability to concentrate. It's just that the ability to concentrate when you need to, or the power to generate the level of intensity needed varies based on your ability to turn it on. I've observed many of the "I can't concentrate" players when they're playing a computer game or involved in some other activity — and they were highly focused for lengthy periods of time. They *can* concentrate! They just haven't learned the skill of turning it on and off when needed during a game.

In this chapter we'll examine the term concentration, and then, keeping with the theme of the book, I'll present actual exercises you can do to improve your concentration.

What is concentration?

Webster's dictionary defines concentration several ways. Two of the definitions are appropriate for our purposes. The first explains concentration as the "direction of attention to a single object." Another more complete definition describes it as a "narrowing or focusing of one's attention on a specific task to the exclusion of all others." I've also heard it defined as "a relaxed state of being mentally alert." I think Costner's "clear the mechanism" is just as appropriate and is one most players can relate to since you've probably experienced it at some time or another.

Regardless of the definition, it is important to bear in mind that concentration is a skill and, like all skills, you can improve it with practice.

You must be present to win!

One of my colleagues and good friends, Dr. Jerry Braza, authored the book *Moment by Moment: The art and practice of mindfulness training*. The original title of the book was *You Must Be Present to Win*. (I use it here with his permission.) Together we discussed mindfulness many times over the years, and I still tell him the original title was more appropriate — especially as mindfulness relates to sports. "Being present" is actually the ability to focus on the task at hand — the task you are currently engaged in — with complete concentration.

Think of the last time you were lost in something you enjoyed doing. You were in the moment. When you are in a state of deep concentration, all your inner chatter is blocked. All that non-stop restless flow of thoughts, all your worries, all anxiety, all that self-talk that persistently runs through your mind — all of it is suspended when you are 100 percent in the moment. You are present. *That's* concentration

— being lost in the moment with no extraneous thoughts. Times when you were "locked in," "in the zone" or "in the groove" were probably the times you played at your best.

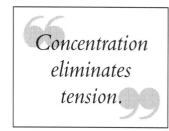

This is also the state when you perform effortlessly. Everything is smooth. You play without tension. Concentration eliminates tension because your mind can only focus on one thing at a time — such as the catcher's mitt or seeing the ball out of the pitchers hand — and all inner chatter is suspended and mechanical thoughts are stopped.

There are multiple ways of developing this skill. Keep in mind that the ability to concentrate and the intensity that works best for you will differ from player to player. Some players perform best if they remain "locked in" for lengthy periods of time during a game, while others reach their best by turning it on and off during the game or even during an at bat. Regardless of how it works best for you, it's important to your success to direct this skill and to be able to alter intensity as needed.

A player with great concentration skills possesses the following traits:

1. Ability to instantly concentrate when needed without thought.

2. Ability to alter the intensity as needed.

3. Ability to focus as long as needed (duration) to stay in the flow of the game.

Improving Concentration: Four Sample Techniques

There are many different ways to improve your ability to concentrate, and I'll present several in this chapter. Anytime you practice something with focus, you improve your ability. All four of the skills outlined in this book — relaxation, affirmation, recall and rehearsal — if done with focus, will improve concentration, especially relaxation.

Besides placing you into the alpha state, relaxation — when done correctly — has the additional advantage of increasing your focus. In the relaxation chapter, I emphasized the importance of not allowing your mind to wander but instead focusing on the feelings within your body — feelings such as heaviness, warmth, your beating heart — or perhaps focusing on specific body parts, which you did in the sequential technique. All of these are means of practicing concentration as long as you do not let your mind wander.

As you will notice, several of the techniques place you in a deeply relaxed state, an almost sleepy state. Such deep relaxation is necessary because it is more difficult to maintain your focus in a fatigued state. By practicing in this state, when it is most difficult, you'll be able to concentrate more easily when you are more alert. Master your mind, don't let your mind master you!

1. Counting Technique

The first technique is quite simple. You just count from 1 to 10 in your mind, one number per exhalation. Then count backward. Repeat the word "in" as you inhale and the number as you exhale. For example "in" (as you inhale), "one" (as you exhale), "in (as you inhale), "two" (as you exhale), etc. Continue for 2, 3, 4 minutes or longer. Continue as long as you can without losing track. You'll notice that over time you'll be able to do it for longer and longer periods.

2. Sequential Breathing

This is a variation of the sequential relaxation technique presented in Chapter 7. In this form you will use your mind to move through your body in sequence: right foot, left foot, right lower leg, left lower leg, right thigh, left thigh, buttocks, trunk, right arm, right hand, left arm, left hand.

The first time through, you feel each part "sinking down" as you exhale (only when you exhale). Do one breath for each body part, then move on with the next body part with the next exhalation. Use only one breath per body part. You want to concentrate on each exhalation to feel the sensation. Next, repeat the entire sequence feeling heaviness in each body part on each exhalation for each body part. On the next rotation, feel warmth. On the next rotation, feel a tingling sensation. Lastly, scan through your body slowly searching for a pulse point.

Use the sequence listed because each sensation you search for will be more difficult to feel than the previous one — you need to increase your concentration. Again, don't let your mind wander or drop off to sleep.

3. Reinforcing Concentration with Mental Skills

Practicing the four-step technique you learned to alter your beliefs should be one of the first things you do to change any behavior. To improve concentration, use what you learned in this book — activate your subconscious mind to reinforce this goal.

I've provided a sample affirmation you can use within the 4-step approach to impress on the subconscious that you have the ability to concentrate — and to do so at the proper times. As emphasized throughout this book, you'll want to develop your own affirmations, and a space is provided for you to do so or to adapt the sample provided.

Your Turn
Affirmation for Concentration

Sample Affirmation: "I am confident, relaxed, focused and in control."

Your Affirmation: _____

_____

_____

Directions:

- Find a comfortable position.
- Focus on your exhalations (or do a relaxation exercise) until you feel relaxed.
- Repeat your affirmation once on each exhalation for 5-6 breaths.
- Visualize a time in the past when you were confident. Feel now what it felt like, then (recall) remember how you walked, your body language on the field, how you interacted with your teammates in the locker room, etc.
- Take that positive feeling and project it into the future. Imagine yourself tonight interacting like you did in the recall with teammates. Feel the way you walk confidently to the mound or from the on deck circle to the plate. Picture yourself focused and attacking the strike zone or being confident, patient and dominant at the plate. Throw the perfect pitch or drive that ball into the gap, etc. (Rehearse with the positive feelings from recall.)
- Flex, stretch and open your eyes, feeling confident, energetic and determined.

4. Standard Autogenic Training

As I've mentioned in previous chapters, the most effective technique I've come across to improve your ability to concentrate is called Standard Autogenic Training (SAT). In the 1970s, I was working with the U.S. Olympic Ski Team, and during a competition in Thunder Bay, Ontario, I met a coach who had defected from behind the Iron Curtain. At that time the Russians and East Germans were years ahead of the U.S. in the theory and practices of mental training. SAT was the foundation skill they used with all the athletes in their programs.

SAT is a very regimented technique that must be implemented exactly as described to achieve maximum benefits. When implemented correctly over a six-week period, the ability to concentrate, both in duration and intensity, can double, triple or even quadruple. In addition, you can expect to not only heighten your ability to concentrate, but also gain all the benefits derived from relaxation.

SAT involves doing three sets, three times a day to acquire the desired benefits. You can use this technique to place yourself in the alpha state and, after doing the last of the three sets, you can implement your mental skills (affirmations, imagery). I will confess that this is not a technique for all players. It requires a tremendous amount of self-discipline to implement this program correctly because during the first two weeks, which focus on improving duration of concentration, each set requires 10-12 minutes or 30-36 minutes per day.

In week three, the sessions begin to hone in on the intensity of focus, and during weeks three through six, each week gets shorter until, by the seventh week, each set takes approximately 2 minutes (or 6 minutes a day) to keep your concentration ability sharp.

Because the description of how to implement SAT is so lengthy, I have included it in the Appendices. Players who are interested in this advanced technique will find it in Appendix B.

In sum...

- We all have the ability to concentrate.

- Concentration means being present, completely focused on the task at hand, to the exclusion of all others.

- Concentration clears your mind. Inner chatter is stopped and this eliminates tension, negative thoughts and thoughts about mechanics.

- You can improve your ability to concentrate because it is a skill, and as a skill it can be practiced.

CHAPTER 14

The Mental Game for Injured Players

"These are the times that try men's souls."

Thomas Paine

Nowhere in the sport of baseball will your mental toughness be challenged more than when you are faced with an injury — especially when confronted with long-term rehab. Unfortunately, injuries are part of the game, and it is a challenge to deal with them and remain positive. Meeting this challenge requires all of your will power, patience, optimism and persistence, applied to both your physical rehab as well as your mental approach to the situation.

Injuries not only cost you playing time, they also pose a major emotional test for any player. Anger, frustration, lack of patience, fear, boredom and depression are just a few of the possible emotions you may experience. Controlling these negative emotions requires that you set new goals and maintain a positive outlook in spite of the challenges you may face. As you search for a silver lining, remember — this time away from the game may be just the time you need to focus on improving your performance when you return.

There is a silver lining in every situation, but when it comes to injuries, finding anything positive in the face of a setback will require some creativity on your part. Your first reaction may be to wonder or worry about the worst-case scenario. That's why it's important to remain calm, step back, and size up the situation.

Try to downsize your injury so that you don't let it get blown out of proportion. Put a plan together by deciding to take ownership of your thinking. That may be all you can control initially, so anticipate the best-case scenario rather than the worst case. Determine to remain positive and to get yourself mentally prepared for the challenges ahead. If you haven't already, begin a gratitude journal, and begin searching for the hidden opportunity that's available within this challenge. This could be a great time to work on your mental game and strengthen it so when you return to the field you are mentally stronger and can perform at a higher level than when you left. View the challenge as an "opportunity in disguise."

Three Ways to Use the Mental Game When Injured

Here are three ways you can use your mental game to aid healing and get prepared for the post-injury phase of your career.

1. **Use imagery to aid the healing process.** The mind is powerful, and research illustrates that imagery can aid the healing process. I've worked with players who cut their projected return date by 20 to 50 percent when they incorporated imagery into the healing process. Your subconscious mind operates your autonomic nervous system, so use it to work for you rather than against you.

2. **Use affirmations to maintain a positive mindset.** Researchers at the Mayo Clinic and other research institutions have found that people who remain positive heal more quickly than those who get depressed. Depression releases chemicals into your bloodstream that actually depress your immune system and slow the healing process. A positive mindset, on the other hand, releases chemicals that strengthen the immune system and aid in healing. Take ownership of your recovery and commit to controlling what you can control.

3. **Use the four-step program to maintain your skill level so you can actually come back playing better than before the injury.** Research again points out that through imagery you can improve physical performance, even without playing or practicing the physical skill. I had my first opportunity in baseball because of an injury to Paul Molitor, as noted previously, that placed him on the disabled list. He took control and used the four basic steps to affirm and visualize playing. He imagined playing in each night's game and took actual "game at bats." He returned to the line-up, playing better and more consistently than he did before he was placed on the DL and began his 39-game hitting streak the first night back. He succeeded, and so have many others I've worked with — using their creative minds to improve physical performance while sidelined.

I'll briefly explain each of these three ways to use the mental game when injured, and I'll provide suggestions on how you can face

Paul Molitor: 39-Game Hitting Streak

I was given my opportunity in baseball because of an injury. Tom Trebelhorn, then manager of the Milwaukee Brewers, convinced Harry Dalton to allow me to work with Paul Molitor in June of 1987.

At that time Paul was injured and was being placed on the DL prior to the All-Star break to give him adequate time to heal. He went on the DL on June 24th and came off following the All-Star break on July 17th.

I met several times with Paul and introduced him to "The Mindset for Winning: A 4-step program for athletes" that I had published earlier that year. Trebelhorn had read the portion of the book describing how players not able to perform physically can "stay sharp" by doing a combination of affirmations and imagery.

During whirlpool treatments, Paul would practice the four steps: relaxation, affirmation, mental recall and mental rehearsal. He would visualize that night's game as if he was playing. He'd faced most of the pitchers that the Brewers were facing and would visualize each pitch, how they would pitch him and what he would do. He'd lay off certain pitches and drive others for hits. Over the 17 days off he was able to bat .1000.

Paul began his 39-game hitting streak, the fourth longest in modern day baseball, on his first night back from the disabled list. He didn't need time to "get into the groove" or to get his rhythm or timing back because he'd never lost it. Too often those thoughts of "it'll take me time to get back" end up being self-fulfilling prophecy.

During his hitting streak, he'd raised his average from .319 to .359. I want to point out that I had nothing to do with his streak other than to introduce him to some current concepts on the mind/body relationship. Paul did what 95 percent of players couldn't do, and that was discipline himself to work diligently toward his goals. His mental toughness and persistence eventually carried him to Cooperstown — and baseball's Hall of Fame.

Imagery to Aid the Healing Process

The goal of using imagery in healing is to increase blood to the injured site. When injured, the body typically constricts (narrows) the blood vessels around the injured site, which slows down blood flow as well as nutrients to the area. At the same time, removal of waste products from the area is hindered. Relaxation coupled with imagery can increase this flow of blood, speeding up the removal of waste and the delivery of oxygen and nutrients, all of which aids the healing process.

Over the years I've worked with many athletes who have used this combination of imagery and relaxation to speed up the healing process. In one instance, a pitcher had an unusual and devastating elbow injury and had less than a 10 percent chance of ever pitching again. He used this combination successfully to return to the major leagues within 18 months. I should mention that he had used imagery successfully in his game and was a believer in the power of the mind. This belief is critical since the subconscious works on the self-fulfilling prophecy concept.

Your Turn

Any deep relaxation technique will improve blood flow to the extremities, where injuries are most likely to occur. The long breath technique, which is explained below, is a very effective in altering blood flow directly to the injured site even if it is not in an extremity. For example, say you have an injured lower back and want to reduce the pain, remove tension in the muscles around the injured area, and improve circulation. All three can be accomplished with the long breath.

Long Breath

1. Perform basic relaxation until you are in a deeply relaxed state. Breathe in as you normally would through your nose/ mouth.

2. Next, inhale normally and imagine the air flowing through your body and visualize it flowing down and out through the injured area.

3. Feel the injured area relax, let go of tension, and feel warmth in this area as you imagine exhaling through it.

4. Continue this sequence for 3-6 minutes or longer. With practice, you'll be able to feel warmth as well as a release of

tension as you exhale. When you can feel the warmth, you are increasing the blood flow.

In/Out Technique

This is similar to the long breath technique except you simply imagine breathing in and out of the injured area.

1. Inhale normally and imagine the air coming in through the injured area, circulating around it and collecting the tension.

2. Then, when you exhale, picture the tension flowing out of your body at the same site.

3. Repeat: Inhale, collect the tension. Exhale the tension out and relax. Inhale, collect the tension. Exhale the tension out and relax. Inhale, collect the tension. Exhale the tension out and relax. Continue for 3-6 minutes or more.

Affirmations to Maintain a Positive Mindset to Aid Healing

I've emphasized throughout this book that you can consciously control the thoughts that enter your subconscious mind and that these thoughts affect your habits, attitudes and behaviors. Controlling your thought process is especially critical during rehabilitation if you want to heal more quickly and actually improve your skill level even while not playing the game physically.

It's easy to be negative. It doesn't require any effort because the situation itself is negative. You can easily get bored with the routine of rehab, spend all of your free time in a hotel room — not to mention spending time around other injured players, some of whom may be negative and depressed. The fact remains that you control your destiny. You can take charge and decide to use this time in a productive manner, or you can go the self-pity route. Get bitter or get better — the choice is yours.

Sample Affirmations

Listed below are some affirmations for injured players that you can adapt. Use the affirmation and reflection process or adapt them to the four-step approach as you see fit for your situation.

Sample Affirmations for Remaining Positive

"I am patient and work hard in my current environment to improve my skills. I will return to the field at the top of my game when my rehab is completed. I know that getting down or depressed will slow the healing process; therefore, I choose to control my thoughts and keep them positive at all times. By keeping positive, I am utilizing my mental facilities, which aid in the healing process. I focus on the present and enthusiastically do everything I can to live each day to the fullest. I realize how blessed I am with both my talent and my current station in life."

"I begin each day with a positive attitude and a plan to improve myself as a person as well as a player. While rehabbing, I look for opportunities to reach out to others who may need a helping hand. I do everything I can to support my teammates and fellow rehabbers in their struggles, and I remain positive so that the environment is a pleasant one."

"Because I am patient, confident, and trust in God, I can focus on the present and improve as both a person and a ballplayer — leaving the future to God. Each day I come to the park enthusiastic and positive with a specific goal for that day, so that I am doing my job in improving my God-given talent. I reach out to others to help them remain positive and live a life of joy, peace and harmony."

Sample Affirmations for Healing

"My body is a powerful healing machine."

"I am healthy, confident, positive and in control at all times. I awake each morning looking forward to today's activities. I come to the park enthusiastic, and I focus only on the positive things that happen. My arm (leg, back, etc.) is strong, healthy, and feels great. Each and every day it gets stronger and stronger. I look forward to many full seasons of health and growth as a ballplayer."

"My _____ is strong and healthy and is getting stronger and healthier each and every day. I feel increased blood flow going to my _____, and this increased blood is bringing in healing nutrients and carrying out any waste from the injury. I feel this healing energy flowing throughout my body as I get stronger and stronger."

See the affirmation chapter for additional samples.

Your Turn

Write several affirmations for healing or for remaining positive when injured:

1. _____

2. _____

3. _____

The Mindset for a Winning 4-Step Program

Recovery is an excellent time to improve your skills mentally. This is the area that most athletes struggle with because it requires incredible self-discipline. Your physical rehab is scheduled, and you are required to do it at the schedule prescribed. The mental game is not scheduled, so it's easy to forget, and it often becomes a lost piece of the puzzle.

Research supports the use of imagery (done properly) to improve your skill level even when you are not physically performing that skill. As discussed previously, your mind can't tell the difference between a real and an imagined experience. When you visualize an activity, your body performs the movement (subliminally) and lays a pattern for increased muscle memory.

Implementing the four basic steps while you're injured is a great way to complement your rehab, keep yourself positive, and prepare both physically and mentally for returning to action. In fact, when you're injured, I'd suggest you mentally engage in actual game situations daily as described in previous chapters. Imagine being in that night's game and performing exactly how you would want to perform if you were actually playing.

In sum...

- Dealing with injuries, especially long-term rehab situations, may be one of the most difficult challenges you face as a player.

- It's important to stay positive and search for opportunities to improve as a player and as a person during this down time.

- A positive attitude assists in the healing process while a negative attitude leads to a depressive state for your immune system, thus releasing chemicals that slow the healing process.

- Goal setting, affirmations and visualization are effective tools to help you stay positive, aid in the healing process and improve your physical skills even when not performing physically.

EPILOGUE

Carpe diem!
(Seize the day!)

APPENDIX A

Psychological Development Form (PDF)

Instructions: In the assessment column, rate yourself on each characteristic. Use a 10-point scale, where 10 is strong, 5 is average, and 1 is weak. In each row, give comments as to why you gave yourself the rating you did, as well as behaviors that must be addressed to improve. Remember, this form is simply a tool to assist you in developing a strategic plan to grow as both a person and a professional baseball player.

Topic	Assessment/ Comments	Goals	Strategy/Plan for Development
Attitude			
Effort (work habits)			
Mental Toughness			
Ability to Focus (concentrate)			
Ability to Relax			
Ability to Deal with Stress			
Self-Concept			
Self-Discipline			
Commitment			
Coachability			
Responsiblity for Actions			
Goal Setting			

Attitude: Your state of mind and approach to life, positive or negative.

Effort: Your desire to give 100% on a day-to-day basis in all areas of development.

Mental Toughness: Your ability to meet and overcome adversity.

Ability to Focus and Concentrate: Can you focus complete attention on the task at hand or do you wander from the goal?

Ability to Relax: Your ability to control muscular tension level as needed for peak performance.

Ability to Deal with Stress: Do you use stress as a positive force (stress as a challenge) rather than allowing stress to control you? Are you able to live in the present without constant worry about the past or the future?

Self-Concept: Your perceived feelings and beliefs about yourself, which determine your behaviors.

Self-Discipline: The ability to control your thoughts, emotions and actions and to control emotional swings.

Commitment: The ability to dedicate yourself to change.

Coachability: Your openness and willingness to listen and learn from coaches as well as to understand instruction.

Responsibility for Actions: Your willingness to assume personal responsibility for your actions without rationalizing behavior.

Goal Setting: Your ability to set realistic goals and adapt goals appropriately. Compatibility of your goals with team goals.

Standard Autogenic Training (SAT)

This technique is by far the best technique I've ever found to improve concentration. It works on increasing both intensity and duration of concentration. It was developed by J.H. Schultz in the early 1900s in Germany, and it reflects the German culture of that time, requiring extreme discipline to complete the 6-week program as outlined.

Benefits

The first two weeks focus on teaching you to concentrate for longer periods of time. Then in week three it shifts to increasing your intensity. As you move to weeks four, five, and six, you learn to change your focus instantly with a high intensity. What athlete wouldn't benefit from all three of these skills?

Prepare Yourself

SAT contains a total of six different exercises designed to train your *body* and your *mind* to respond to your commands.

Each phase of SAT gets progressively harder to perform and thus requires greater concentration. In addition, each phase is added to previous phases, meaning you will be more relaxed as you add each step. As you become more relaxed, you will also find it more difficult to concentrate because you will have a greater tendency to allow your mind to wander or to drift into sleep. To achieve maximum benefits *do not allow your mind to wander at any time!*

The Six-Week Program

I suggest the following guidelines to achieve the maximum benefits from your time spent doing autogenic training:

1. You can perform your affirmations and visualization in conjunction with SAT. Perform all three repetitions of SAT before you perform the mental training (i.e., positive affirmations, mental recall and mental rehearsal) if you connect the two into one session. Instead of using one of the other relaxation techniques, use the SAT for the relaxation component.

2. You want to connect the phrase (affirmation) with the feeling in SAT. For example, when you affirm in your mind, "My right arm is heavy," you should feel the heaviness in the right arm as you exhale. Feeling the sensation is important — that's how you improve your focus because with each step the sensations will get more difficult to feel.

3. Remain alert throughout each practice session. If at any time you are feeling too relaxed or too tired and cannot remain alert, take a deep breath, flex/stretch and come back to an alert state before doing the mental training.

4. Feel the sensations you are searching for on the *exhalation phase of your breathing cycle only.*

5. Log each practice session.

Caution!

Standard Autogenic Training is *not for everyone!* Many people consider SAT a form of self-hypnosis. Although most people see self-hypnosis as positive, not everyone views it that way. If you have any reservations at all regarding the technique, do not use it. Or if you encounter any problems with it, discontinue it.

Keep in mind that SAT is not needed to derive the benefits of mental practice. The other techniques presented will help improve concentration as well, just not as much as SAT.

Step One: Heaviness

Phrase to be used: "My _____ is heavy."

For six breaths (and exactly six breaths, not five or seven), say to yourself, "My right arm is heavy." As you do so, you should feel the heaviness in your right arm during the exhalation phase of your breathing cycle. Time your phrase or thought with your breathing cycle so you can feel the heaviness in the right arm as you exhale.

On the seventh breath, switch your attention to your left arm and use the phrase, "My left arm is heavy." You then feel the heaviness in the left arm for a total of six breaths.

You then move to the right leg for six breaths and on to the left leg for another six, each time changing the phrases accordingly. Then flex, stretch, and open your eyes. Immediately, you repeat the entire sequence a second time, come out of it, and then repeat it a third time.

At the end of the third repetition, perform your mental training (affirmations, recall and rehearsal).

Suggestions for Success

1. When first learning SAT, count each exhalation to make sure you're doing six breaths for each repetition. For example, "One, my right arm is heavy; two, my right arm is heavy, etc." After several days of practice, the counting will not be necessary. You will automatically stop after six breaths because five or seven will not "feel" right.

2. Concentrate so that you feel the heaviness on the exhalation phase of each breath. You can feel the heaviness anywhere in the limb. For example, you may feel it only in a fingertip or you may feel it in the entire hand or the entire limb. Even if you have trouble feeling heaviness or cannot feel it initially, *do not go on for any extra breaths — use six breaths only.*

3. If you begin to feel extreme heaviness or an uncomfortable heaviness, change the phrase to "My _____ is comfortably heavy."

Training Sequence: Week One

Each session includes the following:

First Repetition

"My right arm is heavy." 6 breaths

"My left arm is heavy." 6 breaths

"My right leg is heavy." 6 breaths

"My left leg is heavy." 6 breaths

Flex, stretch, and open your eyes.

Second and Third Repetitions

Repeat entire sequence above a second time, and then repeat the entire sequence a third time.

Step Two: Warmth

Phrase to be used: "My _____ is warm."

Starting on the eighth day, you will shorten the time spent on heaviness and add warmth to the sequence. Warmth will be more difficult to feel but if you've practiced daily, you will have no trouble feeling the warmth relatively quickly.

Training Sequence: Week Two

First Repetition

"My right arm is heavy." 1 breath

"My left arm is heavy." 1 breath

"My right leg is heavy." 1 breath

"My left leg is heavy." 1 breath

"My right arm is warm." 6 breaths

"My left arm is warm." 6 breaths

"My right leg is warm." 6 breaths

"My left leg is warm." 6 breaths

Flex, stretch, and open your eyes.

Second and Third Repetitions

Repeat the above, and follow the third repetition with mental practice if you choose to.

Step Three: Heartbeat

Phrase to be used: "My heart is strong and regular" or "My heartbeat is strong and calm." When you repeat this phrase, feel your heart beating in your chest.

During this step, the previous steps are going to be shortened. Heaviness should be felt in both arms on one breath, then in both legs on the second breath. This requires you to focus your attention on each arm very quickly during that one breath. Warmth will also be shortened to one breath per limb.

Training Sequence: Week Three

First Repetition

"My arms are heavy." 1 breath

"My legs are heavy." 1 breath

"My right arm is warm." 1 breath

"My left arm is warm." 1 breath

"My right leg is warm." 1 breath

"My left leg is warm." 1 breath

"My heartbeat is strong and regular." 6 breaths

Simultaneously flex, stretch and open your eyes.

Second and Third Repetitions

Repeat above sequence.

Step Four: Breathing

Phrase to be used: "It breathes me." Passively observe your breathing cycle and breathing rate while you exhale.

The "it" is your body. Just allow your body to breathe by itself while you focus on the breathing. This will carry you into a very deeply relaxed state. As you add this step, you will once again shorten the previous steps. Each repetition will now require much less time but greater concentration on your part. For example, as you say, "My arms and legs are heavy," you move your mind and attention from right arm to left arm to right leg to left leg, feeling heaviness in each — *all during one exhalation.* Then immediately move to warmth and do the same. You are now feeling in one breath what took you 24 breaths early in the training.

Training Sequence: Week Four

First Repetition

"My arms and legs are heavy." 1 breath

"My arms and legs are warm." 1 breath

"My heartbeat is strong and regular." 1 breath

"It breathes me." 6 breaths

Flex, stretch, and open your eyes.

Second and Third Repetitions

Repeat the above a second and third time.

Step Five: Internal Warmth

Phrase to be used: "My solar plexus is warm." Feel warmth in the internal portion of the trunk of your body (behind the heart, in front of the spine).

All previous steps will be shortened to one breath each when Step Five is added. As you repeat the statement or the phrase, feel the warmth for a total of six breaths for each repetition of SAT. This will follow the previous four steps during each practice session as illustrated below.

Training Sequence: Week Five

First Repetition

"My arms and legs are heavy." 1 breath

"My arms and legs are warm." 1 breath

"My heartbeat is strong and regular." 1 breath

"It breaths me." 1 breath

"My solar plexus is warm." 6 breaths, then flex, stretch and open your eyes.

Second and Third Repetitions

Repeat the above sequence a second and then a third time.

Step Six: Cool Forehead

Phrase to be used. "My forehead is cool." Feel coolness on the forehead while you repeat this phrase on the exhalation. (NOTE: I have found that this step is uncomfortable to some people. If the cool forehead bothers you, disregard this last step and go to the section following week six titled "When Training Is Over: Using SAT".)

Training Sequence: Week Six

First Repetition

"My arms and legs are heavy." 1 breath

"My arms and legs are warm." 1 breath

"My heartbeat is strong and regular." 1 breath

"It breaths me." 1 breath

"My solar plexus is warm." 1 breath

"My forehead is cool." 6 breaths

Flex, stretch and open your eyes.

Second and Third Repetitions

Repeat above.

When Training Is Over: Using SAT

After you've completed the sixth week of training, you will now use a total of 6 breaths for each set. Imagine — it will take you a total of 18 breaths for all three sets. Compare this to the 86 breaths you needed in week two when you were beginning the training.

To maintain the focus intensity you've developed during training, it is important to continue to work on concentration. One way to do so is to use SAT as the relaxation phase of imagery on a regular basis. Another is to use it occasionally (at least 2-3 times a week) while using other techniques on the off-days.

I also recommend that each off-season, six weeks prior to spring training you repeat the entire training process. Rarely do players continue with their daily program during the entire off-season. You do need a break from it just as you do from everything else. And, just like doing PFPs, taking ground balls and working on the basics in spring training to get back to where you were at the end of the season, the mental game needs to be revisited.

APPENDIX C

Mental Recall Worksheet

What game will you be recalling? _____

Experiences and Sensations Felt Prior to that Game

Emotions/Feelings_____

Level of Confidence _____

Thoughts _____

Energy/Stress Level _____

Temperature_____

Smells_____

Sounds _____

Expectations and Goals _____

Others _____

During the Actual Game (what you experienced at various stages of the game or part of the game you are recalling)

Emotions/Feelings_____

Kinesthetic Sensations Felt _____

Level of Confidence _____

Thoughts _____

What You Saw (from your own eyes) _____

Smells_____

Sounds _____

Temperature_____

Others _____

After the Event You Recalled

Emotional Feelings _____

Thoughts _____

Level of Confidence _____

Stress Level_____

Other Things You Experienced _____

Additional Comments and Observations About the Recalled Event

_____

_____

_____

_____

_____

_____

_____

_____

_____

_____

_____

_____

_____

_____

_____

_____

_____

_____

BIBLIOGRAPHY

The following bibliography includes not only the books used in writing this one, but also recommended books that I feel would be helpful to you to further exploring the inner game. This is also a way of thanking various authors whose works have influenced me on my quest of the inner game.

Assaraf, John and Smith, Murray. "The answer." New York: Atria Books, 2008.

Canfield, Jack with Switzer, Janet. "The success principles: How to get from where you are to where you want to be." New York: HarperCollins Publishing, 2005.

Covey, Steven. "The seven habits of highly successful people (workbook)." Covey Leadership Center, Inc., 1995.

Curtis, John. "The mindset for winning: A four-step mental training program to achieve peak performance for all athletes." La Crosse, WI: Coulee Press, 1991.

Curtis, John. "The mindset for winning coaches manual." La Crosse, WI: Coulee Press, 1991.

Curtis, John and Detert, Richard. "How to relax: A holistic approach to stress management." Mountain View, CA: Mayfield Publishing Company, 1981.

Curtis, John. "Learn to relax: A 14-day program." La Crosse, WI: Coulee Press, 1991.

de Mello, Anthoney, SJ. "The song of the bird." Colorado Springs, CO: Doubleday Religious Publishing Group, 1984.

Dorfman, H. A. "Coaching the mental game: Leadership philosophies and strategies for peak performance in sports—and everyday life." New York: Taylor Trade Publishing, 2003.

Dorfman, H. A. "The mental ABC's of pitching: A handbook for enhanced performance." South Bend, IN: Diamond Communications, Inc., 2000.

Dorfman, H. A. and Kuehl, Karl. "The mental game of baseball: A guide to peak performance." South Bend, IN: Diamond Communications, Inc., 1989.

Gallwey, Timothy W. "The inner game of tennis: The classic guide to the mental side of peak performance." New York: Random House Trade Paperbacks, 2008.

Kiefer, Michael Monroe. "The powermind system: Twelve lessons on the psychology of success." Edina, MN: Kiefer Enterprizes International Press, 1995.

Mack, Gary with Casstevens, David. "Mind gym: An athletes guide to inner excellence." New York: Contemporary Books, 2001.

Martin, James, SJ. "The Jesuit guide to almost everything." New York: Harper One, 2010.

Murphy, Jim. "Inner excellence: Achieving extraordinary business success through mental toughness." New York: McGraw Hill, 2010.

Murphy, Joseph. "The power of your subconscious mind." New York: Prentice Hall Press, 2008.

Murphy, Joseph (revised by McMahan, Ian D.). "Think yourself rich: Use the power of your subconscious mind to find true wealth." Paramus, NJ: Reward Books, 2001.

Newman, James. "Release your brakes." Del Mar, CA: The Pace Organization, 1977.

Ortberg, John. "If you want to walk on water, you've got to get out of the boat." Grand Rapids, MI: Zondervan, 2001.

Selk, Jason. "10-minute toughness: The mental training program for winning before the game begins." New York: McGraw Hill, 2009.

Tice, Louis with Steinberg, Alan. "A better world, a better you." Engle Woods Cliffs, NJ: Prentice Hall, 1989.

"Zen Buddhism." Mount Vernon, New York: The Peter Pauper Press, 1959, p. 36.

About the Author

J ack Curtis, a former college coach and athlete, received his PhD in health sciences from the University of Utah. A professor emeritus at the University of Wisconsin-La Crosse, he has more than 35 years' experience working on the inner game with college, national, Olympic and professional athletes in all sports.

His main focus for the past 16 years has been professional baseball, spending 14 years training major- and minor-league athletes and coaches in the Seattle Mariners and Milwaukee Brewers organizations. He is beginning his third season as the mental skills coach for the Philadelphia Phillies, focusing on developing prospects in their minor league system.

Certified as a sports hypnotist by the National Guild of Hypnotists, "Dr. Jack" has authored twelve books on mental skills for athletes and coaches, stress management and health science. He is president of J & K Curtis & Associates, Inc. a professional consulting firm that focuses on helping athletes improve consistency, break out of slumps, challenge their comfort zones and move to a higher level of performance. He can be contacted through the website **baseballs6thtool. com.**

Made in the USA
Charleston, SC
26 April 2012